the Shape
of
Scriptural
Authority

the Shape of Scriptural Authority

David L. Bartlett

FORTRESS PRESS / Philadelphia

COPYRIGHT © 1983 BY FORTRESS PRESS

Library of Congress Cataloging in Publication Data

Bartlett, David Lyon, 1941–
  The shape of scriptural authority.

  Includes bibliographical references and indexes.
  1. Bible—Evidences, authority, etc. I. Title.
BS480.B356 1983   220.1'3   83–48009
ISBN 0-8006-1713-4 (pbk.)

K117D83 Printed in the United States of America 1–1713

For Carol
with my love

Contents

Preface

For some years I was privileged to divide my time between ministry in a local parish and teaching New Testament studies in a university divinity school. My desire to integrate the two aspects of my career reflected larger issues for the two communities. Within the church we constantly asked how the biblical tradition could continue to be the fundamental resource for Christian faith and service in a time apparently so remote from the biblical times. Within the divinity school we wondered how ancient texts, fascinating in their own right, might also serve as Scripture for communities of faith. In both contexts we wondered what the historical and literary study of the biblical texts had to do with the need of church folk for faithful preaching, honest ethical reflection, and growth in discipleship.

As I puzzled over these issues, I was intrigued by some suggestions made by Professor Paul Ricoeur at a colloquium for faculty and graduate students in the theology field at the Divinity School of the University of Chicago. In his paper, later published as "Toward a Hermeneutic of the Idea of Revelation" (in *Essays on Biblical Interpretation,* ed. Lewis S. Mudge [Philadelphia: Fortress Press, 1980], 73–118), Ricoeur argued that the biblical literature does not present a single notion of "revelation" but that the different genres of biblical literature make different claims to revelatory power.

Starting with Ricoeur's suggestion, I tried to examine some of the various kinds of biblical literature to see what claims the texts made for themselves. I shifted the focus of the discussion from the question of "revelation" to the question of "authority." In that way I hoped to focus directly on the texts and their use in communities of faith without being drawn into the difficult and somewhat separate questions regarding a doctrine of revelation. So, too, I largely put aside any discussion of "inspiration" in order to look at the texts themselves and the ways in which they do and should function authoritatively in the church.

Those who read Ricoeur's stimulating essay will note that he describes two forms of biblical literature which I do not discuss, hymnic literature and prescriptive literature. Initial attempts to consider psalms and laws within this study raised so many unresolved questions that I have chosen either to deal with this biblical literature later or not at all. My own addition to Ricoeur's list of the forms of biblical literature is the literature of "witness." Ricoeur talks about witness in the larger context of a "hermeneutics of testimony" (*Essays on Biblical Interpretation*, 119–154), but it seemed to me that some account needed to be taken of the more "personal" literature of the Bible and especially of the epistles. I am grateful for Paul Ricoeur's encouragement in this project, and for the suggestions and criticisms he and Andre LaCocque offered as we discussed my work together.

The third chapter of the book profited especially from the suggestions of students in the course on the Gospels given in Spring 1980 at the Divinity School of the University of Chicago. Chapter 6 profited from the helpful suggestions and bibliography provided by Professor James Barr and from the insights of the seminar on Canon at Chicago, including those of its most distinguished visitor, Amos N. Wilder.

I have tested portions of the book in lectures or seminars at Denison University, Catawba College, Kalamazoo College, and at the First Baptist Church, Dayton, Ohio; Calvary Baptist Church, Denver, Colorado; and Northshore Baptist Church, Chicago, Illinois.

I am grateful for the encouragement of the Divinity School of the University of Chicago where Deans Joseph M. Kitagawa and F. I. Gamwell urged me on and for the support of the Hyde Park Union Church, Chicago, and the Lakeshore Avenue Baptist Church in Oakland.

My colleagues at Chicago also proved to be my teachers, and those who know their work will recognize their influence. I owe a particular debt to my colleagues in New Testament—Hans Dieter Betz, Robert M. Grant and, of honored memory, Norman Perrin and Samuel Sandmel.

Phyllis Berger and Rehova Arthur helped type early portions of this work, and Martha Sheaffer typed the final manuscript carefully and suggested revisions wisely. John Hollar of Fortress Press has nurtured this project from its conception to this final form, and I have profited greatly from his excellent help.

My greatest debt is acknowledged by the dedication.

Abbreviations

Int.	*Interpretation*
JAAR	*Journal of the American Academy of Religion*
JBL	*Journal of Biblical Literature*
LXX	Septuagant
OTL	Old Testament Library
RP	Religious Perspectives
SBLDS	SBL Dissertation Series
SJT	*Scottish Journal of Theology*
SNTSMS	Society for New Testament Studies Monograph Series
TDNT	G. Kittel and G. Friedrich, eds., *Theological Dictionary of the New Testament*
TToday	*Theology Today*
WMANT	Wissenschaftliche Monographien zum Alten und Neuen Testament
ZAW	Zeitschrift für die alttestamentliche Wissenschaft

the Shape
of
Scriptural
Authority

1 / Authority in the Bible

Many Christians think it either odd or inappropriate to raise the issue of biblical authority. Some Christians, for instance, think that appeals to biblical authority are archaic and outmoded. Just as reasonable people are supposed to understand the world and their place in it without appeal to other people's versions of the truth, so reasonable believers are supposed to find for themselves what they can say of God and God's relationship to humankind. No appeal to "authority," however ancient or venerable that authority may be, can dictate to the modern Christian what he or she should believe.

Other Christians think that to raise the question of biblical authority is to question the cornerstone of valid faith. Rightly to believe is to believe what is taught in the Bible, and to question the absolute validity of any biblical teaching is to throw the whole enterprise of faith into danger. The problems which modern people may have with the Bible are a sign of their own pride, their own unwillingness to receive in humility what the Bible has to offer.

Yet some appropriate understanding of the nature of biblical authority seems inescapable for contemporary Christian people. Modern Christians are still modern *Christians*. They belong not only to themselves but to a community of faith and practice, the church. What makes the church a community includes what its members have in common. What Christians have in common includes that body of literature we call the Bible. Christian communities are held together in part by their willingness to appeal to that Bible as having authority for Christian faith and practice.

Modern Christians, however, are also *modern*. Even those Christians who most resist raising the question of biblical authority suggest the importance of the question by the vehemence with which they deny its validity. We are engulfed by understandings of the world and of the self which do not easily fit with the biblical picture or pictures. New insights into the working of the world and the working of the human mind make it difficult to affirm that the Bible tells us all we know about ourselves, or all we need to know. The line between traditional "biblical" self-understanding and contemporary secular understandings does not simply divide Christians from others; it marks a division within the consciousness of the

1

individual Christian. We cannot in good faith pretend that we do not have the questions which we have.

Therefore, the purpose of this book is to discuss anew the problem and nature of biblical authority. I hope to suggest some ways in which Christian people and Christian communities who acknowledge their modernity and its problems can continue to use the Bible as an authoritative resource for their faith and action.

THE NATURE OF AUTHORITY

The very idea of authority is repugnant to many Christians. Authority suggests coercion, the idea that some person or institution can tell another person what to believe or what to do. Authority in this sense is closely related to our pejorative description of someone or some establishment as "authoritarian." Some versions of biblical authority *do* verge on the authoritarian. This authoritarian understanding of the Bible is evident whenever one Christian seeks to end an argument by the simple reminder of what "the Bible says" or decides a complex ethical issue by flipping a Bible open to a proof-text as if there were nothing more to be said.

There is, however, a more positive understanding of authority which is also more appropriate to our discussion of biblical authority. One can talk not only about authoritarian personalities but also about authoritative texts, or sources, or resources. Authoritative resources are not coercive figures who dictate answers and actions. They are rather those resources to which (or to whom) we appeal to provide guidance, or to settle arguments. Among philosophers Wittgenstinians argue about the somewhat cryptic writings of Ludwig Wittgenstein, not only because they disagree about what he wrote, but because they think that what he wrote, rightly understood, provides fundamental clues about the way people talk and think. Platonists are often concerned with deciding what Plato really meant not only because of their scholarly interest in Plato, but because they assume that Plato, rightly understood, helps us rightly understand the world. Lutheran pastors and theologians spend considerable effort seeking to understand Luther because they feel it necessary to test their own claims by what he said. Shakespeare scholars debate some of the apparent incongruities in *Hamlet,* not just because they are there, but because a right understanding of the play may help contemporary actors and directors to stage the play more accurately. (Whether there is the further hope that *Hamlet* rightly played will help the audience better understand life rightly lived lies beyond the purposes of this chapter.)[1]

Analogously, to say that the Bible is authoritative for Christian folk is not to say that the Bible coerces belief or demands obedience. Rather it is to say that the individual Christian seeks rightly to read the Bible as an authoritative resource, an essential guide for faith and practice. More than that, Christian believers and Christian communities discuss issues, seek together, and debate with one another on the basis of Scripture.

When we say that Scripture is authoritative for believers and churches in this way we make two claims.[2] First, Scripture *does* in fact function authoritatively among Christians. It is, in fact, that resource to which Christians and Christian churches appeal for discussions of faith and practice. Second, Scripture *should* function as a fundamental resource for Christians. It is altogether appropriate that Christians appeal to Scripture as an essential guide for their faith and practice and as grounds for discussion and decision.[3]

The purpose of this book is to suggest some of the various ways in which Scripture can appropriately function authoritatively in believing communities. Implicit in this description is the claim that in diverse ways Scripture should have such authority for believing communities as well.

THE NATURE OF SCRIPTURAL AUTHORITY

Typically, the way to discuss the question of scriptural authority is to look at Scripture as a single entity, "The Bible," and to find some external reason for claiming, or denying, the Bible's authority.

Certain Christians affirm the authority of Scripture by appeal to a claim which is not itself contained in Scripture, the claim that the biblical books (at least in their original and inaccessible autograph forms) are inerrant. That is, these Christians claim, one can find no contradictions within Scripture and no contradictions between it and the "facts" of nature and human nature.

Paul Achtemeier judiciously indicates the way in which this commitment to inerrancy functions in practice:

> Obviously, if inspiration is understood to mean inerrancy, then to find error in Scripture is to have misunderstood or misinterpreted it. Conservatives are clear in their own mind that the "plain and obvious" meaning of a text, when found, will bear out the nature of Scripture as error free. For that reason it is wrong to characterize conservatives as "literalists," as though they insist on an absolutely literal interpretation of the text . . . What is at issue is not the literal but the *intended* meaning of the text. In actual practice, the task of conservative interpretation is not to find the literal meaning, but rather to find that interpretation which allows one to continue to affirm the errorless nature of the passage, and of Scripture in general.[4]

Behind this concern with the inerrancy of Scripture is often the assumption that Scripture was divinely dictated by God through the Holy Spirit and that the human "authors" of Scripture were only scribes, recording the divine dictation. So, for instance, B. B. Warfield defined inspiration as the "extraordinary, supernatural influence (or, passively, the result of it) exerted by the Holy Ghost on the writers of our Sacred Books, by which their words were rendered also the words of God, and, therefore, perfectly infallible."[5]

This understanding of Scripture is "external" to Scripture itself in two ways: (1) It presents a doctrine of inspiration which Scripture itself fails to maintain.[6] (2) It takes one form of biblical literature, the prophetic oracle, and assumes that all biblical literature conforms to that norm.[7] In the next chapter we shall examine carefully the nature of prophetic literature in the Bible, but already here we can say that to take Scripture itself seriously as Scripture one needs to acknowledge that the prophetic oracle is not the only kind of biblical literature and that not all biblical literature should be interpreted as deriving its authority from that model.

Other Christians test the authority of Scripture by appealing to different authorities outside of Scripture itself: contemporary philosophy, a modern world-view, "scientific" knowledge of their own, or personal experience. As already suggested, it seems unavoidable for contemporary Christians to be influenced and informed by a whole range of claims not based on a reading of the Bible, claims from their own experience, from the perspective of their culture, or from various "secular" disciplines. Indeed in the discussion of wisdom literature and ethical decision (chapter 4), I shall suggest that such "secular" material also finds affirmation in some biblical literature. However, there are two problems with the appeal to one's own experience or one's modernity as a test for Scripture's authority. First, the very notion of scriptural authority may be sacrificed. To say that Scripture is authoritative is to say that its perspective tests our other perspectives and is not simply tested by them.

Second, if experience is the final authority for faith and practice, it is hard to know how we can hope for Christian *community*. The experience of individual Christians, to say nothing of the experience of Christian congregations in cultures as diverse as Zaire, Japan, and Illinois, is so varied that it is hard to know what grounds there could be for conversation, decision, arguments, and concerted action among Christians. Scripture, however, can and should provide a common source for reflection and appeal.

More helpful than either the appeal to doctrines of verbal inerrancy or the final appeal to contemporary experience is the attempt of some theologians to suggest a richer, more diverse understanding of inspiration than the doctrine of verbal inerrancy would allow. The discussion of these authors focuses less on the specific interaction between the Holy Spirit and the author of a particular book and focuses more on the faith of the communities (Israel, the church) out of which the Bible grew.

> If it is true, therefore, that the church, by its production of Scripture, created materials which stood over it in judgment and admonition, it is also true that Scripture would not have existed save for the community and its faith out of which Scripture grew. That means that church and Scripture are joint effects of the working out of the event of Christ. The close tie between community and Scripture has a most important consequence for our thinking about the inspiration of that Scripture. It is this: if Scripture is to be understood as inspired, then that inspiration will have to be understood equally in terms of the community that produced those Scriptures. Inspiration, in short, occurs within the community of faith, and must be located at least as much within that community as it is with an individual author.[8]

The explication of inspiration is an essential and helpful enterprise in the current discussion. Again, however, it moves outside the scriptural literature itself to find an external center for discussion—here the doctrine of inspiration, or the reconstruction of what happened *behind* the actual writing and editing of the biblical sources: how was the community inspired? Furthermore, discussions of inspiration tend to treat Scripture as a whole: what does it mean to say that Scripture is inspired?

By focusing on the question of *authority* we are able to do two things more effectively than the discussion of inspiration allows. We are able to look at the biblical texts themselves to see what sort of authoritative claims they make—how they function authoritatively in the life of the community. This does not require a doctrine of inspiration, nor, for the most part, does it require a reconstruction of the history lying behind the writing and editing of the texts. Further, we are able to acknowledge the diversity of the biblical texts and to suggest that the types of authoritative claim made by one type of literature (for example, prophetic literature) may not be appropriate in discussing the authority of another (for example, narrative).

This brings us, therefore, to my own program for the discussion of the authority of Scripture in the church. My reflections on the nature of scriptural authority have been greatly influenced by Professor Paul Ricoeur's essay, "Toward a Hermeneutic of the Idea of Revelation."[9] Ricoeur bemoans the monolithic idea of biblical revelation which requires believers to accept a single, propositional definition of biblical faith, a definition which has been filtered through the concerns and the claims of churchly authorities. Instead Ricoeur wants to suggest that a return to the originating texts of faith themselves, to the text of Scripture,"places reflection before a *variety* of expressions of faith, all modulated by the variety of discourses within which the faith of Israel and then of the early church is inscribed. So instead of having to confront a monolithic concept of revelation, which is only obtained by transforming these different forms of discourse into propositions, we encounter a concept of revelation that is pluralistic, polysemic . . ."[10] Ricoeur then goes on to distinguish several sorts of scriptural discourse and to discuss the varieties of "revelation" which these imply. (He also acknowledges that the term "revelation" is really modeled on the discussion of prophetic discourse. Our concern with "authority" may provide somewhat more flexible categories for discussing the variety of biblical genre.) The forms of discourse he discusses are: prophetic discourse, narrative discourse, prescriptive discourse, wisdom discourse, and hymnic discourse.

Using Ricoeur as a starting point, I propose to look at several of the major kinds of biblical literature, to suggest the kinds of authority these forms of literature claim—explicitly or implicitly—for themselves, and to suggest how these authoritative claims might be acknowledged, tested, and affirmed in the lives of believers and of believing communities.

In some ways this approach is close to what James Barr categorizes as the "functional" definition of biblical authority.[11] We shall not, however, simply be discussing the way different biblical texts *do* function in the lives of believers and communities. We shall be discussing the ways in which they ought to function. We shall be discussing those claims for authority which the texts make for themselves, and the ways in which this authority can be tested, affirmed, acknowledged, or experienced by believers.

A word of caution is perhaps appropriate here. The great Christian interpreters of Scripture have in general rightly insisted that the authority of any biblical text is not self-evident, but that the acknowledgement of that authority depends on the testimony of the Holy Spirit.[12] To describe the variety of biblical literature and the various claims to authority that the Bible makes is not to guarantee that the Bible will be read or heard authoritatively. Such authoritative reading and hearing is always a gift of God through faith and to faith, as John Calvin insisted: "These Christians who wish to prove to unbelievers that Scripture is the Word of God are acting foolishly for only by faith can this be known."[13]

And yet the Spirit works in diverse ways and testifies to diverse promises. It is not inappropriate, therefore, to discuss the varieties of biblical literature, to seek to understand the kinds of authority they claim for themselves, to anticipate the ways in which the Spirit may work for believers, and to assume some kind of congruity between the literature of the Bible and the experience of contemporary believers.

PROBLEMS TO BE ADDRESSED

First, there is the problem of the nature of authority. That is, Christians who claim to speak most vigorously for the authority of Scripture often do so on the basis of arguments which do not themselves derive from Scripture, or which do so in only the most tenuous and tendentious way— arguments about direct verbal inspiration and inerrancy.

Second, there is the problem of treating the Bible as if it were all of one literary type. Most often the model for such interpretation is prophetic literature, and the implicit assumption of defenders of biblical authority is that as God gave oracles to the prophets, so God delivered oracles by dictation to the evangelists, the authors of the Hebrew Bible narratives (e.g., of Abraham, Moses, Saul, David), the composers of the Psalms, and the writer of the Book of Job. Again such an argument is extra-biblical in that it fails to do justice to the reality of the Scripture itself and to the diversity of its discourse and of the claims portions of Scripture make for themselves.

Third, there is the problem of our apparent distance from the Bible and the various ages and worlds out of which it arose. What do we have in common with Amos, a herdsman from Tekoa of the eighth century B.C., or with Paul, a traveling apostle from Tarsus of the first century A.D.? Dennis Nineham quotes Dame Helen Gardner, who cites the difficulty of bridging historical distance in a different context:

> It is difficult enough to enter imaginatively into anyone else's religious experience. When two thousand years and more of history separate us from authors and audience it seems rash indeed to imagine oneself viewing a Greek tragedy in the brilliant spring sunshine all those centuries ago. Responses that seem natural and obvious today might not have occurred to me then and elements I now overlook or regard as conventional might then have aroused in me deep religious experience. We necessarily project into the past our own concerns and our own way of seeing the world. Our concepts of the past are historically conditioned.[14]

Fourth, there is the problem of apparent incompatibilities, incongruities, or contradictions in the biblical literature. Can John be correct in saying that Jesus cleansed the Temple at the beginning of his ministry while Matthew, Mark, and Luke place the Temple cleansing at the end of that ministry? Can Matthew be correct in saying that Jesus rode two beasts at the triumphal entry while the other Gospels note only one donkey? Is Luke correct in having Jesus appear to the disciples in Jerusalem after the resurrection while Matthew and Mark place (or promise) such appearances in Galilee?

Fifth, there is the problem of contradictions between biblical literature and what we know, or think we know, in other ways. Is our understanding of evolution (to cite the standard case) compatible with biblical claims about creation? Or, what if careful reconstructions of the settling of Canaan by the Hebrews suggest that a handful of Hebrews were aided by a number of inhabitants of the land to overthrow the ruling orders, and this over a long period of time?

Finally, there is the problem, or the gift, of contemporary theological and ecclesiastical diversity. Theologies and churches with quite different viewpoints and practices claim to base their beliefs and practices upon Scripture. Can we adjudicate among such claims, or do we simply accept the fact that a diverse canon leads to diverse theological and ecclesiastical interpretations and manifestations?

These problems are complex, and no essay will solve them all or any of them completely. But to attend properly to the biblical literature itself, to see what kind of literature it is, to understand what sorts of claims it makes for itself, may put us on the road to a richer and more adequate understanding of biblical authority.

NOTES

1. For a further discussion of the nature of "authority" and "norm" cf. James Barr, *The Bible in the Modern World* (New York: Harper & Row; London: SCM Press, 1973), 23.

2. Cf. Schubert M. Ogden, "Sources of Religious Authority in Liberal Protestantism," *JAAR* 44/3 (1976):405, on *de facto* and *de jure* authority.

3. James D. Smart, *The Strange Silence of the Bible in the Church* (Philadelphia: Westminster Press, 1970), 90. Smart convincingly argues that the authoritative use of Scripture in the churches has fallen off dramatically in recent years. Nonetheless one gets the impression that most Christians and Christian preachers feel that they *should* at least consider Scripture as they seek self-understanding and direction.

4. Paul Achtemeier, *The Inspiration of Scripture* (Philadelphia: Westminister Press, 1980), 56.

5. Quoted in Jack B. Rogers and Donald K. McKim, *The Authority and Interpretation of the Bible: An Historical Approach* (San Francisco: Harper & Row, 1979), 336.

6. For an extended argument, cf. Achtemeier, *Inspiration,* 73–74.

7. Cf. Achtemeier, *Inspiration,* 29, 74 and the discussion of Paul Ricoeur, pp. 5–6.

8. Achtemeier, *Inspiration,* 116. For another excellent treatment, cf. Bruce

Vawter, *Biblical Inspiration* (Philadelphia: Westminster Press; London: Hutchinson, 1972). For an historical treatment of the understanding of inspiration which points toward the centrality—especially within the Reformed tradition—of a more communal understanding, cf. Rogers and McKim, *Authority and Interpretation of Bible.*

9. Paul Ricoeur, "Toward a Hermeneutic of the Idea of Revelation," in *Essays on Biblical Interpretation,* ed. Lewis S. Mudge (Philadelphia: Fortress Press, 1980), 73–118.

10. Ricoeur, "Toward a Hermeneutic," 75.

11. Barr, *Bible in Modern World,* 32–34.

12. Cf., for example, Rogers and McKim, *Authority and Interpretation of Bible,* on Luther, 87; Calvin, 331; Augustine, 26.

13. John Calvin, *Institutes of the Christian Religion,* I, vii, 3, as quoted in Rogers and McKim, *Authority and Interpretation of Bible,* 331.

14. Dennis Nineham, *The Use and Abuse of the Bible* (New York: Barnes and Noble, 1976), 25. The quotation is from *Religion and Literature* (London: Faber, 1971), 43–44.

2 / The Authority of Words

For several reasons it seems appropriate to begin our discussion of the various kinds of literature in the Bible by discussing that literature which refers explicitly or implicitly to the words of God. The Old and the New Testament are both pervaded by the claim that God speaks with humankind, and both portray in diverse ways those various figures through whom God speaks. The opening of the Epistle to the Hebrews captures well a fundamental motif of Scripture:

> In many and various ways God spoke of old to our fathers by the prophets; but these last days he has spoken to us by a Son. (Heb. 1:1-2).

Scripture as a whole is often characterized as the Word of God.[1] Recent New Testament study has often seen the "kerygma" of the early church (the early church's "proclamation" or words about Jesus) as the central source for New Testament theology.[2]

Furthermore prophetic discourse tends to be the paradigm used in certain popular doctrines of the inspiration of the Bible. As God dictated divine messages directly to the prophets, so also God dictated the rest of Scripture to those authors chosen to record the holy words. It has already been suggested that such an understanding of God's inspiration and Scripture's authority is inadequate to the diversity of biblical literature, but we certainly need to take the paradigm seriously and need to understand more fully what various biblical texts themselves imply when they claim to represent the "word of the Lord."

Two strains within biblical thought are especially suitable to understanding the authority appropriate to the "word of God"—the prophetic material in the Old Testament and the description of preaching in the New Testament, especially as we find it in the epistles of Paul.

THE WORD OF GOD IN THE OLD TESTAMENT PROPHETIC LITERATURE

THE AUTHORITY OF THE PROPHETIC WORD

In his book *The Bible in the Modern World,* James Barr writes:

> Today I think we believe, or have to believe, that God's communication with the men of the biblical period was not on any different terms from the

mode of communication with his people today. "Inspiration" would then mean that the God whom we worship was also likewise in contact with his people in ancient times, and that in their particular circumstances, in the stage in which they existed, he was present in the formation of their tradition and in the crystallization of that tradition as scripture; but that the mode of contact was not different from the mode in which God has continued to make himself known to men.[3]

Recent research into the nature of prophecy suggests, however, that Barr's limits on the modes of divine communication are perhaps too parochial. Careful studies of the implications of the biblical literature and of the role of prophets and seers in extra-biblical societies, both ancient and contemporary, suggest radically different understandings and experiences of the divine than those common to many contemporary western Christians.[4]

The literature of the Old Testament itself suggests that the prophets were recognized as having a relationship to God which is not easily assimilable into modern categories. They were set apart in their own time and are set apart from ours by the claim that they did speak, quite directly, the word of the Lord.

We can distinguish several elements of the claim to authority and the nature of authoritative proclamation represented by the classical prophets of the Old Testament.

The Call

The prophet saw himself as one called by God to deliver God's words to the people. The nature of that call can be quite clearly specified. What cannot be so easily specified is how far the call narratives have been shaped in some later period—either by the prophet himself, or by his disciples—as a defense of the authenticity of his commission. Whether direct reminiscences or stylized encapsulations of the prophet's career, the call passages indicate something of the understanding of the nature of prophecy in classical Israel.[5]

One classic example of a call narrative is Jer. 1:4–10:

Now the word of the LORD came to me saying,
"Before I formed you in the womb I knew you,
    and before you were born I consecrated you;
    I appointed you a prophet to the nations."
Then I said, "Ah, Lord GOD! Behold, I do not know how to speak, for I am
only a youth." But the LORD said to me,
    "Do not say, 'I am only a youth';
    for to all to whom I send you you shall go,

Be not afraid of them,
for I am with you to deliver you,
says the LORD."
Then the LORD put forth his hand and touched my mouth; and
the LORD said to me,
"Behold, I have put my words in your mouth.
See, I have set you this day over
nations and over kingdoms,
to pluck up and to break down,
to destroy and to overthrow,
to build and to plant."

On the basis of his study of the calls of Gideon and Moses, Norman Habel has isolated several features of the "call narratives," and we shall follow his designation of those features in discussing the implications of Jeremiah's call narrative for our understanding of prophetic literature.[6]

1. The Divine Confrontation, Jer. 1:4. Jeremiah's call comes through a confrontation with the word of God alone. Unlike Ezekiel (1:4–28) and Isaiah (6:1–4) he sees no vision but only hears a word. The stress on the powerful and active word of the Lord is fundamental to Jeremiah's ministry and oracles.[7]

2. The Introductory Word, Jer. 1:5a. The Lord makes clear to Jeremiah that he was consecrated even before he was conceived. The clear implication is that consecration for the prophetic role can only be God's work. The entire purpose of the prophet's being is contained within the plans and purpose of the Lord.

3. The Commission, Jer. 1:5b. Habel translates the verb *ntn* as an English perfect to make clear that Jeremiah's commission is "an accomplished fact": "I *have* appointed you a prophet to the nations."[8] Jeremiah is not presented with a choice but with a decision already made for him.

4. The Objection, Jer. 1:6. The prophet protests his inadequacy for the commission laid upon him. There is never any indication in the prophetic literature that the prophets were chosen for their special virtues, or that anyone could be "competent" enough to be entrusted with the role of God's messenger. Much of the rest of the book of Jeremiah indicates that for the prophet himself the commission was more of a burden than an honor.

5. The Reassurance, Jer. 1:7–8. Both the prophetic responsibility and the divine assurance are present in these verses. The responsibility of the prophet is not to speak out of his own wisdom or eloquence but to be a messenger for God, to speak precisely what is commanded. The assurance

is that in this task, God will be present to the prophet as a deliverer. The prophet belongs quite totally to God. Both the burdensome responsibility and the final comfort rest in that special relationship to the Lord who sends him.[9]

6. The Sign, Jer. 1:9–10. Habel writes: " . . . the symbolic act of Yahweh extending his compelling hand and touching the prophet's mouth . . . provides additional confirmation that Jeremiah was a mediator who could receive the divine 'word' itself."[10] By this action the Lord makes clear that the oracles Jeremiah speaks come directly from God. The scope and authority of Jeremiah's entire ministry is then summed up in the commission: "See, I have set you this day over nations and over kingdoms, to pluck up and to break down, to destroy and to overthrow, to build and to plant."

Another example of the call narrative is found in Isaiah 6:1–10. Again Habel suggests the ways in which this text fits the features of the call narrative he has distinguished.[11]

Isaiah's call, unlike Jeremiah's, includes not only the active word of God but also the great vision of the heavenly assembly (compare Ezek. 1:1—3: 11).

Again it is clear that the prophet does not earn his prophetic role. Isaiah protests his own unworthiness of the vision of the Lord: "Woe is me! For I am lost; for I am a man of unclean lips, and I dwell in the midst of a people of unclean lips; for my eyes have seen the King, the LORD of Hosts" (Isa. 6:5). It is only the forgiveness and cleansing which comes from the Lord through the action of the seraph which prepares Isaiah for his prophetic commission (Isa. 6:7).

The commission itself again makes clear the intimate relationship between the prophet and God. The prophet is one who is sent by God, who goes *for* God to represent God (cf. Isa. 6:8).

What the prophet says is also given by God: "Go, and say to this people: 'Hear and hear, but do not understand; see and see, but do not perceive'" (Isa. 6:9). Whether the oracle of Isa. 6:9–10 is a summary of Isaiah's message through the years or one of those oracles he claimed to receive directly from the Lord, the implication is clear: as the prophet's office and commission are from God, so the words he speaks are in fact the Lord's words.

Therefore both of these call narratives indicate that the prophets claim no personal authority but derive their authority entirely from the one who calls them, commissions them, and sends them. Furthermore, at some points, the words that the prophets speak are not understood to be their own words but the oracles of God. As those commissioned and informed by God, their words are to be heard and acknowledged as binding on their people.

The Message

Two traditions seem to lie behind the great proclamations of the classical prophets. One tradition indicates that one role of the prophet (as in other societies) was to pronounce oracles from God; often the prophet pronounced the oracles in response to specific questions presented to him. Perhaps the clearest example is Jer. 21:1–7:[12]

> This is the word which came to Jeremiah from the LORD, when King Zedekiah sent to him Pashhur . . . , saying, "Inquire of the LORD for us, for Nebuchadrezzar king of Babylon is making war against us; perhaps the LORD will deal with us according to all his wonderful deeds, and will make him withdraw from us."
>
> Then Jeremiah said to them: "Thus you shall say to Zedekiah, 'Thus says the LORD, the God of Israel: Behold, I will turn back the weapons of war which are in your hands and with which you are fighting against the king of Babylon and against the Chaldeans who are besieging you outside the walls. . . . I myself will fight against you with outstretched hand and strong arm, in anger, and in fury, and in great wrath. . . . Afterward, says the LORD, I will give Zedekiah king of Judah, and his servants, and the people in this city who survive the pestilence, sword, and famine, into the hand of Nebuchadrezzar king of Babylon.

Here the oracle which Jeremiah pronounces is delivered in response to King Zedekiah's specific request for some divine word appropriate to his present calamity, the hostilities begun by Nebuchadrezzar.[13]

The other tradition which helps us understand the prophetic declarations is found in the accounts of other messages and messengers. In Gen. 45:9–11, Joseph delivers a message to his father by the mouths of his brothers:

> "Make haste and go to my father and say to him, 'Thus says your son Joseph, God has made me lord of all Egypt; come down to me, do not tarry; you shall dwell in the land of Goshen, . . . and there I will provide for you.' "[14]

The implication of the setting is clear. Joseph delivers to his brothers a message which they are to deliver verbatim to their father. The formula which introduces the verbatim message is, "Thus says your son Joseph." Following the introductory formula, the brothers are to deliver the message in the first person, to their father.

The prophets use this messenger formula for evident reasons. They, like Joseph's brothers, have received a direct message which they are to deliver verbatim to the intended audience. The message itself often begins with a "therefore" (which links it to the preceding introductory material), and "thus says the Lord," which makes clear that what follows is a direct message.

Amos 7:14–17 sets Yahweh's message in the context of Amos' own situation: Amaziah has told Amos to leave Bethel and to prophesy there no more. Amos replies:

"I am no prophet, nor a prophet's son; but I am a herdsman, and a dresser of sycamore trees, and the LORD took me from following the flock, and the LORD said to me, 'Go, prophesy to my people Israel.'
"Now therefore hear the word of the LORD.
You say, 'Do not prophesy against Israel,
and do not preach against the house of Isaac.'
Therefore thus says the LORD:
'Your wife shall be a harlot in the city,
and your sons and your daughters shall fall by the sword,
and your land shall be parceled out by line;
you yourself shall die in an unclean land,
and Israel shall surely go into exile away from its land.'"

The introductory formula of v. 17, "Therefore thus says the Lord," presents the specific message of Yahweh, here a message of judgment. The prophet presents verbatim and in the first person the Lord's message to Amaziah (and the Lord's message for Israel.)

Jer. 9:1–2 (9:2–3 in the English translations) begins with a lengthy soliloquy by Jeremiah on the iniquity of his people. Then v. 7 picks up the direct message from Yahweh with the messenger formula:

Therefore thus says the LORD of hosts:
"Behold, I will refine them and test them,
for what else can I do, because of my people?"

In these two cases, as in much other prophetic literature, it seems fairly clear that the direct message from Yahweh is set in a larger context which is part of the prophetic oracle but which does *not* claim to be a direct message from Yahweh.

In the case of Amos 7, H. W. Wolff suggests that the larger setting of the message has been recorded and shaped by Amos's disciples. Amos himself introduces the message with the quotation from Amaziah in 7:16 ("You say, 'Do not prophesy against Israel, and do not preach against the house of Isaac.'"). The direct message from Yahweh begins with v. 17.[15] In the case of Jeremiah 9, the prophet almost certainly composed vv. 1–5 as an expression of his own despair, and then introduced the direct message from Yahweh in vv. 6–8[16] (English Translations, vv. 1–6; 7–9).

This description of the prophetic material has significant implications for our understanding of the nature of authority claimed by the prophetic genre. To be sure, the model of the prophet as a mouthpiece for God, a direct spokesman for Yahweh's message, is appropriate to some material within prophetic literature, especially that material introduced by the message formulas. However, within the larger body of the prophetic books, and even within the speeches of the prophets themselves, we see a good deal of creative material used to introduce the divine messages. So Gerhard von Rad writes:

> As a rule, however, the prophets prefaced this messenger formula with another form of words whose purpose was to draw the recipient's attention to the message. . . . These two, the messenger formula and the prefaced clause, must both be present before we have the literary category "prophetic oracle."[17]

Therefore the prophet is not only the direct spokesman for God, presenting verbatim the messages he has received, he also creatively provides a setting for that message. The prophetic books represent not only specific dictation from God, they represent the prophet's attempts to set God's dictates within an appropriate context and to present God's dictates in an appropriate literary form. Sometimes they represent the work of the prophet's disciples and later redactors, who placed the oracles into a larger shape and (as in Amos) gave them their appropriate historical context.

"The Word of the Lord"

Von Rad points out that of the 241 times that the phrase "the word of Yahweh" (*dbr yhwh*) occurs in the Old Testament, 221 times the phrase relates to a prophetic oracle.[18] Sometimes, to be sure, the phrase is almost certainly an editorial insertion. Sometimes, too, it refers not simply to the message the prophet has received from Yahweh but to the larger section of material, including the prophet's own reflections (e.g., Jer. 14:1–10). Initially, however, the phrase "the word of the Lord" apparently referred more directly to that message of Yahweh which the prophets were directed to proclaim.

The typical phrase of the prophet Ezekiel, "the word of the Lord *came* to me,"[19] suggests that the prophetic experience had the quality of an event. The prophetic oracle was given by the Lord in a specific moment.[20]

Furthermore the word of the Lord was not simply descriptive or predictive, it was powerful. It could accomplish what it announced. So in Isa. 55:10–11a the prophet presents an oracle from Yahweh:

"For as the rain and the snow came down from heaven,
     and return not thither but water the earth,
making it bring forth and sprout,
     giving seed to the sower and bread to the eater,
so shall my word be that goes forth from my mouth;
     it shall not return to me empty."[21]

According to the Book of Amos, Amaziah tells Jeroboam the King that "the land is not able to bear all (Amos's) words," suggesting that Amos not only predicts Israel's exile and Jereboam's death, but that the words with which he fills the land help to bring those events about (Amos 7:10).[22]

Von Rad points out the completeness which the phrase "the word of the Lord" implies.

It is very significant that the phrase always appears with the definite article, "*the* word of Jahweh," and never in the indefinite form, "*a* word of Jahweh." . . . For however brief and concise the word might be, it was intended as *the* word of Jahweh for the man who received it and for his situation. The word that came on each occasion is not to be set alongside the rest of the words of Jahweh, so that it is only in the synthesis that it yields something like the message the prophet has to announce; on the contrary, for the person concerned it is the complete word of God.[23]

That is to say that each "word of the Lord" is the complete word which the Lord has to speak to that occasion, and each specific occasion provides the opportunity for an oracle which suggests even in its very specificity the broad ranges of God's judgment and God's mercy.

The Prophet and Tradition

Prophetic oracles, their language and their images, did not simply emerge *ex nihilo*. The great prophets borrowed from and interpreted the traditions of their people. The prophet Isaiah drew most heavily upon traditions related to David and to God's establishment of Jerusalem, the city of Zion.[24] The later prophet, whom we call Second Isaiah, drew far more heavily upon traditions related to the exodus.[25] In neither case did the prophet simply repeat traditional material to make a familiar point.

For Isaiah the traditional hope that Yahweh will bless Zion is chastened by the realization that Yahweh may precede that blessing with judgment:

Ho Ariel, Ariel,
the city where David encamped!
Add year to year;
     let the feasts run their round.

Yet I will distress Ariel,
  and there shall be moaning and lamentation,
  and she shall be to me like an Ariel.
And I will encamp against you round about,
  and will besiege you with towers,
  and I will raise siegeworks against you.
Then deep from the earth you shall speak,
  from low in the dust your words shall come;
your voice shall come from the ground like the voice of a ghost,
  and your speech shall whisper out of the dust (Isa. 29:1–4).[26]

For Second Isaiah the return from exile recalls the acts of God in the exodus, but God will not simply conform to the pattern of God's former acts. The people in exile are not simply to look back at Yahweh's former activity, though that has served as a pointer to Yahweh's present aid. They are to acknowledge that Yahweh will do new and even greater things for Yahweh's people:

Thus says the LORD,
  who makes a way in the sea,
  a path in the mighty waters,
who brings forth chariot and horse, army and warrior;
they lie down, they cannot rise,
  they are extinguished, quenched like a wick:
"Remember not the former things,
  nor consider the things of old.
Behold, I am doing a new thing;
  now it springs forth, do you not perceive it?
I will make a way in the wilderness
  and rivers in the desert" (Isa. 43:16–19).

In the exodus, Yahweh made a path through the sea and turned the waters into dry land. In this new and greater event, Yahweh makes a path through the desert, and brings forth waters from the dry land.[27]

Not only do the prophets re-present and re-interpret the great streams of their people's tradition, they pass on motifs of the prophetic tradition itself, often reinterpreting the images they have received. Second Isaiah draws on First Isaiah; Jeremiah apparently draws on Hosea.[28]

Walther Zimmerli points out that in Amos 5:18–20, Amos uses a traditional motif, "the day of the Lord," and radically shifts its meaning to speak to a new situation:

Woe to you who desire the day of the LORD!
  Why would you have the day of the LORD?
It is darkness, and not light. (Amos 5:18).

Then, says Zimmerli, other prophets—Isaiah, Zephaniah, Ezekiel, Joel, Malachi—pick up the motif of the "day of the Lord." They retain, with Amos, the suggestion that the day of the Lord is a day of judgment, but the shape of that judgment and the reasons to expect judgment shift from prophet to prophet, according to the situation in which each prophet lived and the oracles which he received. Something of the surprising and sovereign power of God is indicated in each prophetic use of the motif, but the nuances change from prophet to prophet, century to century.[29]

Therefore while the prophets claim to speak the word of the Lord as delivered to them, to speak as messengers of the Lord, the words the prophets receive and the way in which they shape and present those words rely upon traditions. The prophets do not simply repeat traditions, but they acknowledge them, make use of them, and reinterpret them in the light of new situations and new claims by God.

The Prophet and his Community

Romantic notions of the prophet standing alone, apart from any community of support, have largely given way in recent years to an understanding of the prophet as one who is related to some community which supports him and acknowledges his authority. Early references to pre-classical prophets suggest that prophets sometimes traveled in groups. For instance, Samuel tells Saul that they will meet a band of prophets (1 Sam. 10:5).[30] Obadiah hides a hundred prophets, in groups of fifty, in a cave (1 Kings 18:4). Elijah and Elisha were apparently part of a community of prophets, or sons of prophets, and they acknowledge that Elijah's authority passes to Elisha when Elijah is taken up to heaven (2 Kings 2).

Clearly the preservation of the classical prophetic literature as we have it in Scripture depended upon a group of disciples or adherents of the prophets who saw fit to preserve the prophetic words for future generations. We see evidence of this process in Isa. 8:16–17, where the prophet says:

> Bind up the testimony, seal the teaching among my disciples, I will wait for the LORD, who is hiding his face from the house of Jacob, and I will hope in him.[31]

Baruch undoubtedly played a role in the preservation of Jeremiah's sayings, and the book of Jeremiah is itself probably the result of a complex process of preservation and addition by a wider circle of disciples and interpreters of the prophet.[32]

Robert Wilson argues that studies of "intermediaries," prophet-like figures, in a number of cultures suggest the inevitable importance of a support group for the prophet. Wilson responds to Max Weber's description of the charismatic:

> This reading of Weber has in turn given rise to the popular image of the prophet as a divinely inspired individual who reforms society with his radical message and who refuses to be a part of the corrupt social order that he condemns. . . . The evidence indicates that few intermediaries actually fit Weber's pattern. Many are not leaders, although they do derive their authority from their ability to communicate with the divine realm. Furthermore, they are usually well integrated into their support groups. . . . Most important, intermediaries owe their position ultimately to the validation of their support groups.[33]

All this suggests that the prophets derived their support in part from groups which acknowledged their authority. Furthermore, the fact that a group of followers acknowledged the prophet's authority helped guarantee that the prophet's oracles would be preserved (and expanded and edited) for succeeding generations.

The Prophet as Intercessor

Wilson suggests that one strain of prophetic understanding, that of the "Ephraimite" prophets, draws upon traditions about Moses as a model for its self-understanding. Included in the traditions about Moses is the tradition that he interceded for the children of Israel with God.

Wilson suggests that Jeremiah, for instance, stood within this tradition when he interceded with the Lord for his people. Jer. 21:1–10 represents the request from Zedekiah that Jeremiah intercede for the people, and the Lord's negative response to Jeremiah's intercession.[34] Jer. 7:16 suggests that part of Jeremiah's characteristic role has been to act as intercessor for his people:

> (The word that came to Jeremiah from the LORD).
> "As for you, do not pray for this people, or lift up cry or prayer for them, and do not intercede with me, for I do not hear you."

Amos 7:1–3 (not from the Ephraimite tradition) shows Amos in a similar role:

> Thus the Lord GOD showed me: behold, he was forming locusts in the beginning of the shooting up of the latter growth; and lo, it was the latter growth after the king's mowings. When they had finished eating the grass of the land, I said,
> "O Lord GOD, forgive, I beseech thee!
> How can Jacob stand?
> He is so small!"
> The Lord repented concerning this;
> "It shall not be," said the LORD.

The prophet, therefore, not only speaks for the Lord to Israel and Judah; the prophet also intercedes for Israel and Judah before the Lord.

To summarize the material we have surveyed so far, the prophets are understood in the Old Testament as ones who speak for God. At some points they proclaim the messages of the Lord verbatim, in the first person, as mouthpieces for the God they represent. The words they pronounce represent both the wholeness and the specificity of God's word for the specific situation which the prophet addresses. However, the word of the Lord which the prophet pronounces is often set within a literary context which discloses the imagination and interpretation either of the prophet or of his followers; and this larger context, too, is sometimes called "the word of the Lord." Both the oracles themselves and the literary contexts in which they are set use and reinterpret traditional material—drawn from the stories of Israel and Judah or from the sayings of previous prophets. While the prophets derive their particular authority from the Word of God which they speak, that authority is also acknowledged by a group of disciples which supports them, preserves, edits, and supplements their words. While the prophet is seen primarily as the one who speaks for the Lord to the people, sometimes the prophet also speaks on behalf of the people to the Lord. He is a genuine intermediary.

THE ACCEPTANCE AND VALIDATION OF PROPHETIC AUTHORITY

We now move from the description of prophetic literature to the questions: What sort of authority do the prophetic proclamations claim to have? How did Israel and Judah come to acknowledge some prophets as authentic and authoritative while other prophets were rejected as false? What sort of claims does prophetic literature explicitly or implicitly make for its own authority?

Prophetic Literature as Self-Authenticating

To a great extent, the classical prophets do not offer external proofs of the validity of the oracles which they proclaim. They declare that the word which they speak is a message of the Lord and that therefore they speak neither their own words nor on their own authority. They call their listeners to *hear* that word, which means both to listen to the oracle and to acknowledge its authenticity.[35] The readers are expected to respond there and then, by repenting, by undertaking appropriate action, by waiting patiently upon the deliverance which the Lord will provide. They are not asked to wait and see whether a prophet turns out to be authentic or his prophecy accurate before they are called to respond to the oracles he speaks.

> When you spread forth your hands,
>   I will hide my eyes from you;
> even though you make many prayers,
>   I will not listen;
>   your hands are full of blood.
> Wash yourselves; make yourselves clean;
>   remove the evil of your doings
>   from before my eyes;
> cease to do evil,
>   learn to do good;
> seek justice,
>   correct oppression;
> defend the fatherless,
>   plead for the widow (Isa. 1:15–17).

> "And to the house of the king of Judah say, 'Hear the word of the LORD, O house of David! Thus says the LORD:
> "Execute justice in the morning,
> and deliver from the hand of the oppressor
>   him who has been robbed,
> lest my wrath go forth like fire,
>   and burn with none to quench it,
>   because of your evil doings'" (Jer. 21:11–12).

This word of the prophets not only calls the faithful to repentance, it provides judgment on the unfaithful. To hear and not to believe is to be cut off from the promise and the mercy which the word of the Lord, *in itself*, provides. Thus Isaiah's call includes this oracle from God:

> "Go, and say to this people:
> 'Hear and hear, but do not understand;
> see and see, but do not perceive.'
> Make the hearts of this people fat,
>   and their ears heavy,
>   and shut their eyes;
> lest they see with their eyes,
>   and hear with their ears,
> and understand with their hearts,
>   and turn and be healed" (Isa. 6:9–10).

The prophetic oracles may be termed "self-authenticating" because they do not appeal to any warrant outside themselves for their authority. They do not claim to be "reasonable" or to "fit" general human experience. They speak directly for themselves and rightly to hear them is to acknowledge their truth.

Related to the direct claim to authority which the prophetic word contains is the prophet's desire to base his authority on the call he received from Yahweh. The call narratives we examined may have been told in part (either by the prophet or by the community which followed him) to authenticate the prophet's role as a messenger from God, speaking authoritatively for the Lord.[36]

Prophecy as Fulfilled

I have suggested that the prophetic word not only pointed to God's action but to some extent initiated God's action. Therefore that prophecy was deemed to be authentic which proved to have power, which was fulfilled and enacted.

This real relationship between prophecy and enactment is clear enough in the more immediate historical context of the prophetic oracles.

When Jeremiah tells Hananiah that he (Hananiah) is prophesying falsely, he concludes with this oracle of Yahweh: "Therefore thus says the Lord, 'Behold, I will remove you from the face of the earth. This very year you shall die, because you have uttered rebellion against the Lord.'" The editor of the Book of Jeremiah then adds the note of verification: "In that same year, in the seventh month, the prophet Hananiah died" (Jer. 28:16–17). The prophetic books also claim a kind of historical validity on a larger scale, however. The process of canonization, of deciding what prophets would remain normative for Israel and Judaism, probably included the decision as to which prophets had been sustained by the events of history. While there were undoubtedly many prophets predicting peace and mercy in the period before Judah's captivity,[37] it was Jeremiah who rightly predicted the coming judgment, and his words became part of his people's Scripture. So, too, in the period of the exile, those prophets who foresaw the eventual return of God's people to Zion were sustained by the events of history and their words were preserved in Judaism's canon.[38]

Undoubtedly the process of canonization was a long and complex one. The followers of a prophet probably preserved his oracles in the confidence that he would be seen by succeeding generations as a genuine speaker for God. Other oracles may have been added, along with historical notes. The canonical prophetic books included more material than the original oracles of the prophet and were shaped in ways appropriate to the time in which they were written.[39]

Nonetheless, the decision that certain prophets' words did not return empty was in part a decision made by the believing community over the generations and centuries.

John Bright would argue that the historical vindication has continued
from those early generations until now:

> It is only as men who believed, who *knew* that the word they spoke was the
> word of their God that the prophets are to be understood at all. . . . To
> that, one can add only that their words have in the truest sense been
> vindicated by history. By this one does not mean merely that a great number
> of their predictions demonstrably came to pass, but rather that their words
> have stood the test of time. Though specific words addressed to specific
> situations of the ancient past, they have about them an eternal quality; they
> are enduring words.[40]

True and False Prophets

As I have already suggested, one clue for understanding the authority of
the prophets is found in the biblical accounts of disputes or tensions
between true and false prophets.

The issue of the relationship between true and false prophets is raised
most often and most acutely in the book of Jeremiah. For instance,
Jeremiah encounters Hananiah, another prophet (Jeremiah 28). The issue
between them is whether Judah will be conquered by Nebuchadnezzar.
Hananiah prophesies that Yahweh will bring back the vessels of the temple
from Babylon and that the exiles will return to Jerusalem. He pronounces
this oracle with the traditional and appropriate messenger formula, in the
first person singular, as a verbatim announcement of the Lord.

Jeremiah responds to Hananiah:

> "Amen! May the LORD do so; may the LORD make the words which you have
> prophesied come true, and bring back to this place from Babylon the vessels
> of the house of the LORD, and all the exiles. Yet hear now this word which I
> speak in your hearing and in the hearing of all the people. The prophets who
> preceded you and me from ancient times prophesied war, famine, and
> pestilence against many countries and great kingdoms. As for the prophet
> who prophesies peace, when the word of that prophet comes to pass, then it
> will be known that the LORD has truly sent the prophet" (Jer. 28:6–9).

Hananiah then engages in a sign-act, as he breaks the yoke which
Jeremiah bears on his shoulders, thus indicating that Yahweh will break the
yoke of Nebuchadnezzar which is on the necks of the nations. Jeremiah
goes away and some time later receives an oracle from the Lord.

> "Go, tell Hananiah, 'Thus says the LORD: you have broken wooden bars, but I
> will make in their place bars of iron. For thus says the LORD of hosts, the God
> of Israel: I have put upon the neck of all these nations an iron yoke of servitude
> to Nebuchadnezzar, king of Babylon, and they shall serve him, for I have
> given to him even the beasts of the field'" (Jer. 28:13–14).

Jeremiah then pronounces Yahweh's judgment on Hananiah, prophesying his death within the year, and the editor confirms that in the seventh month of that year, Hananiah died according to the prophecy.

Several motifs are evident in the contrast between Hananiah, the false prophet, and Jeremiah, the true. It is clear, for instance, that there is nothing in the form of the prophecy which distinguishes Jeremiah from Hananiah. Both pronounce perfectly traditional oracles, using the message formula.[41] Nor do we have any indication that Hananiah is corrupt or malicious in his intent.

What is at stake first of all is the simple (but irreducible) question: Does Hananiah speak the oracle of the Lord? Nothing in the story resolves that question until Jeremiah receives an oracle which contradicts Hananiah's. Now, since Jeremiah and the reader knows that he receives true oracles from the Lord, and since his oracle contradicts that of Hananiah, both Jeremiah and the reader know that Hananiah's oracle is untrue; he is a false prophet.[42]

There were two further issues. First, will Hananiah's prophecies come true? Jeremiah acknowledges that if the prophecy of peace comes to pass, that will show the accuracy of Hananiah's claim to be a prophet (Jer. 28:9).[43] Second, does Hananiah stand in the great prophetic tradition? This is not, of course, a conclusive test, but Jeremiah does note that on the whole the prophetic tradition in which he stands has preached judgment rather than peace. There is, therefore, especially good reason to be wary of those who preach peace (Jer. 28:8).

Of course Jeremiah clinches his case by prophesying Hananiah's death, which prophecy is fulfilled. Thereby the reader learns that Jeremiah is a true prophet, and that Yahweh has executed justice on Hananiah.

However, it is clear from the literature in Jeremiah that no external criteria can be cited for assuring the truth or proving the falsehood of a prophet. What makes the true prophet true is that he speaks the Lord's oracle. Beyond the claim (in the true prophet's case the knowledge) that it *is* the Lord's oracle that he speaks, there is nothing he can say. Von Rad sums up the problem and Jeremiah's "solution":

> The very fact that Jeremiah could not point to any criterion that might in principle answer the question—who was the false prophet and who the true—showed him the full difficulty of the problem; for there could be no such criterion in respect of form or content. Just because Jahweh was not "a God at hand" but a God "far off" (Jer. 23:23) there could be no standard method of any sort by which he granted revelation.[44]

The analysis of the disputes with the false prophets further confirms our analysis of the nature of prophetic authority. In the first instance, prophetic speech is self-authenticating speech; that is, it represents the claim of the speaker to speak the message of the Lord, and no external criterion can validate that claim. Secondly, however, the way in which the word points to and initiates activity in history helps to confirm its validity.

Finally, the commitment and faith of the community which preserves, reshapes, and finally canonizes prophecy becomes a kind of popular validation, not within the lifetime of the prophet, but in the economy of God's dealing with faithful people.

THE WORD OF GOD IN THE NEW TESTAMENT

THE AUTHORITY OF PREACHING IN PAUL

The New Testament writer who is most concerned with the authoritative nature of words is the Apostle Paul. In 1 Corinthians he describes his apostolic ministry:

> For since, in the wisdom of God, the world did not know God through wisdom, it pleased God through the folly of what we preach to save those who believe. For Jews demand signs and Greeks seek wisdom, but we preach Christ crucified, a stumbling block to Jews and folly to Gentiles, but to those who are called, both Jews and Greeks, Christ the power of God and the wisdom of God. For the foolishness of God is wiser than men, and the weakness of God is stronger than men (1 Cor. 1:21–25).

At a number of points it is clear that Paul understands Christian preaching in ways strikingly similar to the description of Old Testament prophecy I have presented in the preceding pages.

The Apostolic Call

Though Paul does not claim that all Christian preachers (or prophets) are apostles, in Galatians he does describe his own call to apostleship in terms which not only recall Jeremiah but which are undoubtedly heavily influenced by Jer. 1:5.

> For I would have you know, brethren, that the gospel which was preached by me is not man's gospel. For I did not receive it from man, nor was I taught it, but it came through a revelation of Jesus Christ. . . . But when he who had set me apart before I was born, and had called me through his grace, was pleased to reveal his Son to me [or "in me,"or "by me"], in order that I might preach him among the Gentiles [or "nations," cf. Jer. 1:5], I did not confer with flesh and blood, nor did I go up to Jerusalem to those who were apostles before me. (Gal. 1:11–17; cf. also Rom. 1:1–7).

As with the prophets, Paul can specify a particular time for his call, and relate it to the rest of his life. As with the prophets, it is God alone who calls the apostle to his apostleship. As with the prophets, the apostle's authority lies precisely in the fact that he is sent (authorized to preach the gospel among the Gentiles: the root of the Greek word for apostle is the verb *apostellō,* "I send").

As with the prophets, it is God who gives the apostle the message he is to preach: "I did not receive it from man, nor was I taught it, but it came through a revelation of Jesus Christ" (Gal. 1:12).

In all these ways Paul compares his call as an apostle with the calls of the classical prophets, and insists that he, too, speaks the oracles of the Lord to those people to whom the Lord has sent him, the Gentiles.

The Message

In the writings of Paul we get only indirect evidence of the nature of his actual sermons. He explains why he preaches and alludes to what he preaches, but he does not provide many clear examples of the preaching itself.

When he does refer to his proclamation he tends not to use the prophetic formula "a word of the Lord," but to refer either to "the gospel" (the noun *euaggelion;* the verb *euaggelizomai*) or to "the proclamation" (the noun *kērygma;* the verb *kērusso*). Both these terms (though their Christian use is probably not original with Paul) derive originally from the role of a messenger who presents a proclamation for which he was commissioned.[45]

Certainly Paul sometimes includes the idea of commissioning in his references to his role as evangelist or proclaimer:

> For Christ did not send me to baptize, but to preach the gospel (1 Cor. 1:17).
>
> For if I preach the Gospel, that gives me no ground for boasting. For necessity is laid upon me. Woe to me if I do not preach the gospel! For if I do this of my own will, I have a reward; but if not of my own will, I am entrusted with a commission (1 Cor. 9:16–17).
>
> But how are men to call upon him in whom they have not believed? And how are they to believe in him of whom they have never heard? And how are they to hear without a preacher? And how can men preach unless they are sent? (Rom. 10:14–15a).

Whether or not what the preacher declares is (as with a prophetic oracle) a verbatim message from the Lord, Paul clearly thinks that the preacher is one commissioned, and that the gospel—its content if not its form—is given as part of that commission.

Furthermore, as with the prophetic word, the gospel carries with it its own enactment; it is not only a word but a power. As with Isaiah's prophetic word, the gospel divides the faithful from the unfaithful:

> For the word of the cross is folly to those who are perishing, but to us who are being saved, it is the power of God (1 Cor. 1:18).
> And my speech and my message were not in plausible words of wisdom, but in demonstration of the Spirit and power, that your faith might not rest in the wisdom of men but in the power of God (1 Cor. 2:4–5).

Finally, as J. Christiaan Beker suggests, just as the prophetic word represented the whole of Yahweh's word to a given situation, so Paul's preaching, and by extension his letters, present the whole implication of the Gospel for a particular people in a particular situation:

> Because the letter is eminently particular and occasional, it wants to be a substitute for the dialogical directness of the apostolic word *hic et nunc* and yet claims divine authority and binding revelation, just like the prophetic word and letter in the Old Testament prophetic and apocalyptic literature. . . . The letter form, then, with its combination of particularity and authoritative claim, suggests something about Paul's way of doing theology. It suggests the historical concreteness of the gospel as a word on target in the midst of human, contingent, specificity. . . . Particularity and occasionality do not constitute a contamination of Paul's "pure thought"; rather, they serve to make the truth of the gospel the effective word of God.[46]

The Use of Tradition

It is clear that Paul's proclamation includes considerable use of tradition. His letters are full of citations of the LXX and/or Hebrew Scripture, and we can be reasonably sure that his preaching also relied on the exposition of such texts.

Moreover, in 1 Corinthians 15, Paul makes it clear that the content of the gospel which he preaches includes traditions which he has received from those who were believers before him:

> Now I would remind you, brethren, in what terms I preached to you the gospel, which you received, in which you stand, by which you are saved, if you hold it fast—unless you believed in vain.
> For I delivered to you as of first importance what I also received, that Christ died for our sins in accordance with the scriptures" (1 Cor. 15:1–3).

In 1 Cor. 11:23, Paul says that he received "from the Lord" what is undoubtedly also a piece of early Christian tradition. Whether this account was directly part of his preaching is hard to know.

What is clear is that Paul's sense of apostleship, the claim of a direct commission from God, does not conflict with his use of either the

Scriptures or early Christian traditions in his preaching. His letters also suggest that, as with the prophets, he feels free to interpret those traditions in fresh ways, and to apply them imaginatively to new contexts.[47]

The Apostle as Preacher

As with the prophets, the authority of the apostle may derive from God, but it is also acknowledged by a smaller or larger community of support. In Paul's case we can see him seeking to defend that authority against threats from outside (cf. Galatians, 2 Corinthians).

The fact that his letters have been preserved, then circulated, and finally canonized suggests that a small circle of supporters existed from the beginning, that it expanded, and finally came to include—at least officially—the larger church which recognized the canon.

Like the prophets, Paul not only proclaims the message, the gospel, to the community but he also *intercedes* for the community with God. For instance, Paul sees himself in the pattern of Moses (cf. Exod. 32:32) interceding for Israel:

> I am speaking the truth in Christ, I am not lying; my conscience bears me witness in the Holy Spirit, that I have great sorrow and unceasing anguish in my heart. For I could wish that I myself were accursed and cut off from Christ for the sake of my brethren, my kinsmen by race (Rom. 9:1–3).

Most of Paul's letters include prayers of thanksgiving, which themselves may contain elements of intercession:

> I thank my God in all my remembrance of you, always in every prayer of mine for you all making my prayer with joy. . . . And it is my prayer that your love may abound more and more, with knowledge and all discernment, so that you may approve what is excellent, and my be pure and blameless for the day of Christ, filled with the fruits of righteousness which come through Jesus Christ, to the glory and praise of God (Phil. 1:3–4; 9–11).

In all these ways, Paul's self-portrait as apostle and preacher or evangelist comes remarkably close to the prophet's self-portrait as messenger for God. The major difference seems to be that whereas the prophet receives an oracle directly from Yahweh, the content of Paul's proclamation—given him by the Lord, to be sure—is mediated through the tradition of the church. And while it may speak to a particular audience, as does the prophetic oracle, Paul's preaching centers regularly and constantly in the proclamation of Christ crucified and risen. The center of the proclamation, the oracle if you will, remains constant.

(The discussion of the gift of prophecy in 1 Corinthians 14 suggests that some Christian prophets still received direct oracles which could be communicated verbatim in intelligible speech. This sort of prophecy, however, does not apparently provide the fundamental self-understanding of Paul's apostleship, which rests rather in the commission to preach the gospel whose content is already given and centered in Christ's crucifixion and resurrection.)

THE ACCEPTANCE AND VALIDATION OF THE AUTHORITY OF PREACHING IN PAUL

The Proclamation as Self-authenticating

When Paul deals with false or mistaken apostles, he sounds like Jeremiah trying to deal with false prophets. There are no clear external signs by which to determine who is a true apostle and who is not. What Paul knows is that his apostleship is from God, and therefore anyone who denies that apostleship fails to acknowledge authority which is not human but divinely commissioned.[48]

When Paul deals with mistaken Christian proclamations, what he knows is that his gospel was given him by God, and that any gospel which contradicts it is, therefore, by definition, not gospel at all.

> I am astonished that you are so quickly deserting him who called you in the grace of Christ and turning to a different gospel—not that there is another gospel, but there are some who trouble you and want to pervert the gospel of Christ. But even if we, or an angel from heaven, should preach to you a gospel contrary to that which we preached to you, let him be accursed (Gal. 1:6–8).

> I feel a divine jealousy for you, for I betrothed you to Christ to present you as a pure bride to her one husband. But I am afraid that as the serpent deceived Eve by his cunning, your thoughts will be led astray from a sincere and pure devotion to Christ. For if someone comes and preaches another Jesus than the one we preached . . . or if you accept a different gospel from the one you accepted, you submit to it readily enough (2 Cor. 11:2–4).

Related to this claim of the self-authenticating nature of the gospel is the reminder that the preaching of Christ crucified stands in stark contrast either to signs or to wisdom: it does nor coerce by miraculous show nor persuade by compelling argument. It is received through faith.[49] Preaching, like the prophetic oracle, does not appeal to any standard outside itself by which it may be tested or judged. In that sense it is self-authenticating. It is to be accepted as true on its own terms.

Faith Through Hearing

Closely related to the claim that the gospel carries its own authority is the claim that rightly to receive the gospel's authority is to *hear* the proclamation faithfully. For Paul, rightly to hear the preached word is to acknowledge both its truth and its saving power.

> So faith comes from what is heard, and what is heard comes by the preaching of Christ (Rom. 10:17).
>
> Does he who supplies the Spirit to you and works miracles among you do so by works of the law, or by hearing with faith? (Gal. 3:5).

The Validation of the Spirit

While the proclamation carries its own authority, and that authority is acknowledged only in faithful hearing, nonetheless Paul suggests that that faithful hearing does have consequences in the gifts of the Spirit poured out upon the faithful. In the Old Testament the Spirit often rests upon the proclaimer.[50] In Paul the Spirit is also poured out upon those who hear the proclamation and receive it with faith.

> For I decided to know nothing among you except Jesus Christ and him crucified. And I was with you in weakness and in much fear and trembling; and my speech and my message were not in plausible words of wisdom, but in demonstration of the Spirit and power, that your faith might not rest in the wisdom of men but in the power of God (1 Cor. 2:2–5).
>
> In Christ Jesus the blessing of Abraham (has) come upon the Gentiles, that we might receive the promise of the Spirit through faith (Gal. 3:14).

The nature of those gifts of the Spirit are suggested in the texts of Romans 8, 1 Corinthians 12—14, and Galatians 5. They suggest that while the fundamental validation of the word for Paul is in its faithful hearing, that faithful hearing does have discernible consequences in the life of the believer. The faithful hearers are those who have received the Spirit and its gifts.

HEARING THE WORD OF GOD TODAY

Our discussion of the prophets and of Paul's understanding of Christian preaching suggests that the mode of authority implicit in one genre of biblical literature is its claim to speak a word given by God. That word may be given in an oracle as to the prophets, or it may center on the portrayal of the event of Christ crucified and resurrected as in Paul. It almost certainly will contain an element of tradition, but it will interpret that tradition in novel ways. While the oracle or the proclamation itself may claim to be a message delivered by God, the prophet or apostle will self-consciously and imaginatively set the revelation in a larger literary or epistolary context. The word will not claim to be one part of a larger system of doctrine or one aspect of God's diverse and continuing revelation, but for that moment and that occasion, it will claim to be *the* word of God.

In this way, Scripture claims that some of its passages are therefore to be understood as "self-authenticating." Rightly to hear them or to read them is to acknowledge their authority. We can expand somewhat on that claim, first by looking at the way in which portions of Scripture might claim to be self-authenticating; second by looking at the relationship of Scripture to preaching as a mode of self-authenticating discourse.

SCRIPTURE AS SELF-AUTHENTICATING

Karl Barth has suggested that on the whole, Scripture is to be understood as self-authenticating proclamation—or perhaps more accurately, as proclamation authenticated by the testimony of the Spirit of God to the faithful hearer or reader.[51] For Barth, Scripture is not in any sense "inerrant." It represents those human words by which faithful people declare God's full revelation in Jesus Christ, the Word incarnate. Nonetheless Scripture stands over against our attempts to decide whether or not it is authoritative. It declares its own authority, its own truth, and the reader accepts that authority in faith:

> Scriptural exegesis rests on the assumption that the message which Scripture has to give us, even in its apparently most debatable and least assimilable parts, is in all circumstances truer and more important than the best and most necessary things that we ourselves have said or can say.[52]

It is quite clear that for Barth, the authentic word which Scripture declares of itself is the Word about Jesus Christ. Scripture manifests that preaching which Paul, too, thinks is fundamentally self-authenticating:

> The Bible says all sorts of things, certainly; but in all this multiplicity and variety, it says in truth only one thing—just this: the name of Jesus Christ, concealed under the name Israel in the Old Testament, revealed under His own name in the New Testament, which therefore can be understood only as it has understood itself, as a commentary on the Old Testament.[53]

As this book intends to make clear, we are less sure than Barth that Scripture says only one thing, or at least unsure that it always says the one thing in the same way, so that Scripture can be best understood and appreciated according to a single notion of authority. However, Barth does here delineate that strain of prophetic and apostolic proclamation which is central to Scripture, the strain which declares, "Hear the word of the Lord!"

From a secular literary critic comes a description of certain sorts of literature which provide the criteria by which to judge their own excellence. I shall cite the passage and then explicate its pertinence for our analysis.

> Instead of some final cogent argument demonstrating to the world that *since* S is an absolute standard and *since* work X realizes, it, therefore X is good, we really say, in effect, "I experienced X and found it teaching me the value of that kind of work, which I therefore now value. It also taught me that it realizes that value in high degree—better than others of the kind I know of or can imagine—and *therefore* I know it to be a good member of a 'good kind.'" In short, we judge the work by the values we have learned to employ by reading the work.[54]

Let me illustrate what Wayne Booth seems to suggest. Suppose we are reading *Hamlet* for the first time. The appropriate way to decide its worth is not to begin by defining the rules for a particular kind of work called a tragedy (or a revenge tragedy) but to see the shape, movement, emotions, and convictions which emerge from the play. On the basis of the play a new understanding of the tragic emerges, an understanding which that play powerfully (perhaps uniquely) embodies. On the basis of that new understanding we judge and affirm the play itself.

James Joyce's *Ulysses* caused something of an uproar at its publication in part because it did not fit any of the rules for any genre of literature. Was it an epic or a mock epic or a novel or an extraordinarily long prose poem? The reading of the work confirmed for many people that what Joyce did here he did extremely well, and therefore *Ulysses* became a paradigm for a certain kind of literature. On the basis of standards derived from the reading of *Ulysses,* many critics have deemed it a classic work.

Booth's analysis helps us to understand the self-authenticating nature of some biblical literature. In order that we might rightly hear Jeremiah's oracles, or Paul's proclamation of the cross, we should not approach them with a preconceived set of standards, such as: "What should a true prophet say?" or "What do I already known about God?" or "What has been my own experience of judgment and redemption, or of the lack of either judgment or redemption?" or "What seems empirically verifiable about these claims?" or "How does this accord with positivism, or Marxism, or Freudianism, or any other school to which we happen to belong?"

Rightly to hear Jeremiah's oracles or Paul's proclamation is to realize that they not only provide answers to certain questions but that they also suggest what questions we ought to be posing. They do not so much meet our standards for truth as cause us to redefine our standards for truth.

In his own time, Jeremiah suggested that rightly to hear his oracles was fundamentally to alter the listener's thinking about God and God's dealing with Judah, the nature of judgment and the promise of mercy.

In his own time, Paul made clear (cf. 1 Corinthians 1 and 2) that to *hear* his proclamation of the cross is to redefine one's questions, one's experience, and one's standards for truth. No longer is the demand for signs—external evidences of God's mercy—appropriate. No longer is the search for wisdom—some kind of coherent system of rationally persuasive convictions—adequate. The word of the cross causes the listener radically to reshape his or her questions and to rethink his or her needs. For example, the word may cause the reader or listener not to ask: "How can we find God?" but to affirm: "Here is how God has found us."

To the extent that Scripture is self-authenticating, the way in which we lay hold of its authority, as both Paul and the prophet suggest, is to *hear* faithfully. Faithful hearing means laying aside for the moment those questions and presuppositions we bring to Scripture in order to see what questions Scripture may raise of us. It means assuming for the moment that the word called "the Word of God" is addressed to us in our concrete need and provides us with specific hope. Faithful hearing means being willing to obey the word we receive, when that word provides for us direction for our living and our action.

A simple analogy comes from tales of the sea, at least in their Hollywood version. In adventure movies set on shipboard the climactic moment often comes (when the iceberg is first sighted or safe harbor is sighted at last) as the captain speaks over the loudspeakers: "Now hear this, now hear this!"

The voyager then knows that the word which comes will be a true word, a crucial word ("Go to the lifeboats!"), a word which applies directly to the lives of those who hear. The proper response to such a word is to listen, trust, and act.

Sometimes Scripture speaks to the reader or listener with a "Now hear this!" The word is self-authenticating insofar as it can claim to be a true word, a crucial word, and a word which applies directly to the one who hears. Scripture suggests that the proper response to such a self-authenticating word is to listen, trust, and to act. That is what Paul calls "hearing with faith" (Gal. 3:2).

Our claim that Scripture in some of its modes represents self-authenticating discourse is closely related to recent work on the nature of the classic and of the religious classic in particular.

In his book *The Classic,* Frank Kermode suggests that two clear marks of the literary classic are that the classic continues to be read over a long period of time and that the classic invites a variety of readings. If a work is not open to diverse interpretations it is not sufficiently rich to sustain its interest and value over a long period of time.[55] The two characteristics of durability and multiplicity of possible meanings leads to "the paradox that the classic changes, yet retains its identity. It would not be read, and so would not be a classic, if we could not in some way believe it to be capable of saying more than its author meant."[56]

David Tracy, in his book *The Analogical Imagination,* starts with Kermode's criteria of a classic but further specifies the characteristics of the classic work and of the religious classic in particular.[57] According to Tracy, the classic is not only perduring and multivalent, it is also provocative, true, and the religious classic at least is revelatory as well.

A classic is provoking in that it challenges the perceptions and presuppositions of the reader; "The text can become a classic for the reader only if the reader is willing to allow (his or her) present horizon to be vexed, provoked, challenged by the claim to attention of the text itself."[58] Tracy further refuses to accept any formalist definition of the classic which attributes classic stature to a work without regard to the truth or value of the work's content. "My thesis is that what we mean in naming certain texts, events, images, rituals, symbols and persons 'classics' is that here we recognize nothing less than the disclosure of a reality we cannot but name truth. . . . With an experience that upsets conventional opinions and expands the sense of the possible; indeed a realized experience of that which is essential, that which endures."[59]

For a Christian theologian like Tracy it is not a large step from the claim that the classic provides a realized experience of "that which is essential, that which endures" to the claim that the *religious* classic is revelatory of God. "Unlike the classics of art, morality, science and politics, explicitly religious classic expressions will involve a claim to truth as the event of a disclosure-concealment of the whole of reality *by the power of the whole*—as, in some sense, a radical and finally gracious mystery."[60]

We can see how closely this discussion of the classic relates to our own discussion of Scripture as self-authenticating.

To return to our "secular" examples, I have argued that rightly to read *Hamlet* is not to bring to that play our own criteria for excellence or significance, demanding that the play meet our criteria of worth. Rightly to read *Hamlet* is to let our questions be shaped in part by the play itself. In this sense that classic is, as Tracy suggests, provocative. Because it provokes different readers in different ways and because its very richness of interpretive possibility has ensured its endurance, *Hamlet* provides a classic example of a classic.

By Tracy's standards a further question must be raised: does *Hamlet* disclose to us truth—a richer perception of ourselves and of the human reality? Having attended to *Hamlet* carefully, do we then need to attend to the world in new and newly perceptive ways? If so then *Hamlet* is a classic indeed.

Are Jeremiah's oracles and Paul's proclamation classics, and religious classics? History testifies to their enduring qualities, and the library shelves full of exegetical volumes testify to the fact that both Paul and Jeremiah are open to diverse interpretation, changing even with the changing concerns of human epochs.

We have already argued that part of what makes Paul and Jeremiah "self-authenticating" is their provocative quality, the way in which they cause us to reformulate our questions and shift our presuppositions. We have also argued that both Paul and Jeremiah claim to speak truth, calling upon the reader to "hear" them openly and to respond to them faithfully. In this way, like Tracy's religious classics, they are disclosive of a truth beyond themselves.

Further, the truth to which these religious classics point is the truth of God, perhaps better the true God, what Tracy calls "the power of the whole."

What further needs to be added to qualify the inclusion of Jeremiah and Paul among the religious classics? First the reminder (which Tracy would not deny) that within the large realm of the religious classic further distinctions of genre and function must be made. Both the Gospel of Mark and the oracle of Jeremiah have legitimate claim to be religious and revelatory classics, but they do not reveal in the same way. Mark reveals by the "indirect" route of narrative, by telling a story which in its adumbrations and implications continually points beyond itself. Jeremiah reveals (sometimes at least) by the direct "Thus says the Lord." He reveals by presenting, as a messenger, the divine "Now hear this," not as narration but as dictation.

Related to this is the claim that for Paul's preaching and Jeremiah's oracles the texts claim to point quite directly beyond themselves. Jeremiah's texts are not only Jeremiah's texts, they are God's oracles, and rightly to hear them is not to hear the prophet but quite directly to hear the one who sent him. Paul's sermons (or the fragments which survive) re-enact the power of the cross which for Paul is the central place where God's gracious mystery is quite evidently and publicly revealed. In ways which not many religious classics would claim, Jeremiah and Paul would claim that God speaks and acts and saves and judges quite directly in what they say.

Finally there is the reminder that Paul's and Jeremiah's words (along with the rest of the Bible) are claimed by the church to be not only classic but Scripture. They form part of the canon, and the canon is that body of literature by which even other religious classics are judged. The question whether a work is a Christian "classic" within the context of the believing community is answered in part by asking how congruent that work is with the fundamental classics of Scripture. Indeed within the framework of Judaism and Christianity, most extra-canonical religious classics are held to be classic because they illumine for later generations something of the rich and varied possibilities of Scripture itself.

PROPHECY, PROCLAMATION, AND EXPERIENCE

Our discussion of the prophets and of Paul's preaching also suggests that sometimes the claims of the prophets or the preacher can be enriched, if not tested, by certain kinds of experiential or empirical tests.

For the prophets the question was sometimes whether the prophecy of God's judgment or mercy in fact corresponded to the way in which Israel's or Judah's history proceeded. Jeremiah emerged as a great prophet in part because he rightly perceived that Nebuchadnezzar would be victorious and the exile of the Judeans would not quickly end. II Isaiah emerged as a great prophet in part because the shape of mercy which he foresaw in God's activity in Cyrus was borne out by history (Isa. 44:28—45:7).

Paul claimed that hearing in faith was followed by the experience of the Spirit, and that the Spirit was evident in a variety of gifts, most importantly in the increase of faith and hope and love.

While the fundamental test of the words of God or the proclamation of the cross is their self-authenticating power, a secondary confirmation of their authority is provided by testing them against our own experience, or perhaps better, by rethinking our experience in the light of Scripture.

Does the content of God's mercy and judgment as contained in the prophets correspond to the signs of judgment and the promise of mercy in the lives of believers or the history in which we live? Does the proclamation of Christ crucified and risen, when that proclamation is heard, believed, and obeyed, lead to lives richer in faith, in hope, in love, in purpose?

No prophet or apostle would have wanted to say that the experiential results were the final test of the authenticity of the words proclaimed. But Paul and the prophets did maintain a kind of congruence between the promises of their proclamation and the ways in which faithful people could discern God working in the world. It was not that the listeners were to bring to the prophets or the apostle their own views of history or set of experiences and then see whether the oracle or the sermon fit the listeners' preconceptions. It was rather that, on the other side of the oracle, with their preconceptions changed and their perceptions shifted, the listeners could see that history did point to the judgment or the promise the prophet declared. The listeners could recognize that life seen , or seen anew, in the light of a cross and a victory was life which was more coherent, more promising, and more full.

PREACHING AND THE PROPHETIC MODE

It is clear that the place where the contemporary church most often models itself on the prophets and apostles is in the task of preaching. The preacher does not claim precisely what the prophet claimed. He or she does not claim to have received an oracle direct from God, to be delivered verbatim to its rightful audience. But he or she may claim like the prophet to be one who interprets tradition, who interprets tradition creatively, and who applies that tradition to a new situation. When the preacher makes that claim it is not illegitimate for the preacher to hope and to pray for something of that self-authenticating power which Scripture claims for itself.

The preacher is perhaps closer to the apostles than to the prophets. Paul used both the traditions of Old Testament and the traditions about Jesus, crucified and risen, as the content for his own faithful reflection and creative application of God's word to new situations.

Like both the prophets and the apostle, the preacher's authority derives primarily from the call and message of God, but that authority is also appropriately acknowledged and affirmed by a community, a congregation. Like the prophets and apostles, the preacher who preaches aright not only declares God's Word to the congregation but intercedes before God *for* the congregation. The preacher is God's advocate and the people's advocate as well.

Of course for the preacher, both the prophets and the apostles have become part of that traditional material which is the basis for creative reflection and application. In a sense then, the preacher always stands at a further remove from the initial oracle, or the earliest proclamation of Christ crucified and risen.

Nonetheless, if the preacher believes that God continues to address those who hear faithfully, the preacher can view the sermon as an explication of "the word of the Lord." And the congregation can hope and believe that sometimes the sermon will provide the opportunity for that faithful hearing which Scripture says is the appropriate response to the God who spoke and speaks to humankind.

Of course not all sermons are sermons on prophetic texts or on the apostolic preaching. Nor do all sermons explicate or adumbrate Scripture's "Thus says the Lord." Other sorts of texts suggest other sorts of sermons, as I shall demonstrate, but for the preaching ministry of the church it is the prophets and the apostles who provide the fundamental model.

NOTES

1. One of the central theological achievements of the twentieth century, Karl Barth's *Church Dogmatics* begins with a lengthy exposition of "The Doctrine of the Word of God," though Barth does not therein deal exclusively with Scripture as God's word and in later volumes does not identify Scriptures so directly with the Word of God. Karl Barth, *Church Dogmatics,* I/1 and I/2, Eng. trans. G. T. Thomson and Harold Knight (Edinburgh: T. & T. Clark, 1956).

2. Centrally, of course, this is true of Rudolf Bultmann in his *Theology of the New Testament,* Eng. trans. Kendrick Grobel (New York: Charles Scribner's Sons; London: SCM Press, 1954, 1955).

3. James Barr, *The Bible in the Modern World* (New York: Harper & Row; London: SCM Press, 1973), 17–18.

4. Two especially helpful books, which I shall cite extensively, are Johannes Lindblom, *Prophecy in Ancient Israel* (Philadelphia: Fortress Press; Oxford: Basil Blackwell, 1962); and Robert R. Wilson, *Prophecy and Society in Ancient Israel* (Philadelphia: Fortress Press, 1980). While Gerhard von Rad's *Old Testament Theology,* Vol. II, Eng. trans. D. M. G. Stalker (New York: Harper & Row; Edinburgh: Oliver & Boyd, 1965) does not deal so extensively with extra-biblical cultural parallels to prophetic experience, his careful reading of the biblical literature certainly suggests that Barr's understanding of the mode of communication appropriate to the prophets is anachronistic.

5. On the question of "historicity," cf. George W. Coats and Burke O. Long, eds., *Canon and Authority: Essays in Old Testament Religion and Theology* (Philadelphia: Fortress Press, 1977), 3–20, and von Rad, *Old Testament Theology,* II:55.

6. Cf. Norman Habel, "The Form and Significance of the Call Narratives," *ZAW* 77/3 (1965):297–323.

7. Cf. Habel, "Call Narratives," 307, on the formula "the word of the Lord came to me."

8. Habel, "Call Narratives," 308.

9. For further analysis, especially of the "I am" reassurance, cf. Habel, "Call Narratives," 308–9.

10. Habel, "Call Narratives," 309.

11. Habel, "Call Narratives," 309–12.

12. Cf. Lindblom, *Prophecy,* 149.

13. Cf. Jer. 37:3ff, 37:17; also cited in Lindblom, *Prophecy,* 149.

14. Cf. von Rad, *Old Testament Theology,* II:47; for considerable material on "commissioned communication," see Ann M. Vater, "Narrative Patterns for the Story of Commissioned Communication in the Old Testament," *JBL* 99/3 (September 1980):365–82.

15. Cf. H. W. Wolff, *Joel and Amos,* Hermeneia—A Historical-Critical Commentary on the Bible (Philadelphia: Fortress Press, 1977), 308–16.
16. Cf. John Bright, *Jeremiah,* Anchor Bible (Garden City, N.Y.: Doubleday & Co., 1965), 73.
17. Cf. von Rad, *Old Testament Theology,* II:37; Lindblom, *Prophecy,* 158; Wilson, *Prophecy and Society,* 142.
18. Von Rad, *Old Testament Theology,* II:87.
19. E.g., Ezek. 12:1, 17; 13:1.
20. Cf. von Rad, *Old Testament Theology,* II:68.
21. Cf. Lindblom, *Prophecy,* 117.
22. Cf. Lindblom, *Prophecy,* 120; von Rad, *Old Testament Theology,* II:89.
23. Von Rad, *Old Testament Theology,* II:87–88.
24. Von Rad, *Old Testament Theology,* II:155–69.
25. Von Rad, *Old Testament Theology,* II:239–41.
26. Von Rad, *Old Testament Theology,* I:164.
27. Von Rad, *Old Testament Theology,* II:247.
28. Von Rad, *Old Testament Theology,* I:43.
29. Walther Zimmerli, "Prophetic Proclamation and Reinterpretation," in *Tradition and Theology in the Old Testament,* ed. Douglas A. Knight (Philadelphia: Fortress Press, 1977), 75–76.
30. Cf. Lindblom, *Prophecy,* 65–66.
31. Cf. Lindblom, *Prophecy,* 160.
32. Cf. Bright, *Jeremiah,* lxiii–lxx.
33. Wilson, *Prophecy and Society,* 58; for a somewhat similar point on the importance of socially-recognized authority for a prophet, cf. Burke O. Long, "Prophetic Authority as Social Reality," in *Canon and Authority,* ed. Coats and Long, 3–20.
34. Cf. Jer. 37:3–10; 42:1–22; and Wilson, *Prophecy and Society,* 238.
35. Cf. Klaus Koch, *The Growth of the Biblical Tradition,* Eng. trans. S. M. Cupitt (New York: Charles Scribner's Sons, 1969), 218; similarly, Abraham J. Heschel, *The Prophets* (New York: Harper & Row, 1962), 22–23.
36. Cf. von Rad, *Old Testament Theology,* I:55; somewhat modified by Long, "Prophetic Authority," 11–13.
37. Cf. Jer. 6:13–14.
38. For further reference to this process of canonization, cf. James A. Sanders, "Hermeneutics in True and False Prophecy," in *Canon and Authority,* ed. Coats and Long, 24.
39. Cf. R. E. Clements, "Patterns in the Prophetic Canon," in *Canon and Authority,* ed. Coats and Long, 42–45.
40. Bright, Jeremiah, xxv–xxvi.
41. See the analysis of the form in Koch, *Biblical Tradition,* 207–10.
42. See Jer. 14:14, where Jeremiah receives an oracle from the Lord announcing that other prophets who prophesy in the Lord's name prophesy lies: "I did not send them, nor did I command them or speak to them." Cf. also Jer. 23:25–32. For further examples of false prophets, cf. Lindblom, *Prophecy,* 210.
43. Cf. Jer. 27:10f.
44. Von Rad, *Old Testament Theology,* II:209.

45. Cf. the appropriate articles on these words by Gerhard Friedrich, *TDNT* 2 (1964):707–37; *TDNT* 3 (1965):683–717.

46. J. Christiaan Beker, *Paul the Apostle: The Triumph of God in His Life and Thought* (Philadelphia: Fortress Press, 1980), 24.

47. See, for example, Paul's interpretation of Deut. 30:12–14 in Rom. 10:6–8.

48. See Gal. 1:11–12; 2 Cor. 3:4–6.

49. Cf. 1 Cor. 1:18–25.

50. Cf. Ezek. 11:5; Isa. 61:1.

51. Barth here would be closer to Paul than to the prophets in understanding the content of Scripture and of proclamation not to be so much oracles of Yahweh as the portrayal of Christ crucified and risen. Cf. Barth, *Church Dogmatics*, I/2, 710–40 (esp. 720) for this and much of my basic reading of Barth on Scripture.

52. Barth, *Church Dogmatics*, I/2, 719.

53. Barth, *Church Dogmatics*, I/2, 720.

54. Wayne Booth, *A Rhetoric of Irony* (Chicago: University of Press, 1974), 208.

55. Frank Kermode, *The Classic: Literary Images of Permanence and Change* (New York: Viking Press; London: Faber & Faber, 1975), 117, 121.

56. Kermode, *The Classic*, 80.

57. David Tracy, *The Analogical Imagination: Christian Theology and the Culture of Pluralism* (New York: Crossroad, 1981), 154.

58. Tracy, *Analogical Imagination*, 105.

59. Tracy, *Analogical Imagination*, 108.

60. Tracy, *Analogical Imagination*, 163.

3 / The Authority of Deeds

In addition to that kind of biblical literature which presents and proclaims the words of the Lord, there is another kind which deals with God's deeds. And if one model of scriptural authority relies heavily on the paradigm of prophetic discourse, other models rely heavily on stories which can be interpreted as reports of the acts of God, or on scriptural narrative as the fundamental genre under which other forms of biblical literature can be subsumed.[1]

The narratives of Scripture are not of a piece. Any reader can discern distinctions in implication and tone among such diverse narratives as the temptation of Adam and Eve, Abraham's binding of Isaac, Absalom's betrayal of David, Job's testing, the birth narratives of the gospels, the parable of the lost coin, the accounts of Jesus' crucifixion, and the story of Pentecost. Biblical scholars apply different labels to the stories in order to indicate something of the particular nature of each: myths, legends, sagas, parables, tales, chronicles.

A simpler classification may suffice, at least initially, as we try to understand the nature and peculiar authority of the biblical narrative material. Some of the biblical narratives purport to represent history—actual events within the recorded memory of humankind. Among such narratives we would include the history of Saul, David and the Davidic kings in Books of Samuel and Kings, sections of the gospels, and the Book of Acts. Other biblical narratives make no claim to represent history. They are presented as stories—important stories, authoritative stories, but not as stories which claim to represent an actual event within the history of humankind. Among these we would certainly include such writings as the Book of Job in the Old Testament and the parables of Jesus in the New Testament.

As the rest of this chapter will show, it is much too simple to suggest that the distinction to which we here refer is the distinction between fact and fiction, and many narratives are exceedingly difficult to fit into either of our broad categories with any certainty. However as a beginning to our understanding, the general distinction between historical and non-historical narrative seems a useful one.

HISTORICAL NARRATIVE IN THE BIBLE

A recent biography of Ulysses S. Grant includes the following:

Jesse Grant established his tannery in Point Pleasant (Ohio). Then, at age twenty-seven, he married Hannah Simpson and settled in a small attractive house near the river. . . . There, on April 27, 1822, was born Jesse and Hannah's first child, who was given the name Hiram Ulysses Grant. When the boy was eighteen months old, the family moved to the new town of Georgetown, away from the river and near good supplies of tanning bark.[2]

At first sight, at least the style and function of the narrative is not strikingly different from that of certain biblical material.

And sons were born to David at Hebron: his first-born was Amnon, of Ahinoam of Jezreel; and his second, Chileab, of Abigail. . . . These were born to David in Hebron (2 Sam. 3:2–5).

And Joseph also went up from Galilee, from the city of Nazareth, to Judea, to the city of David, which is called Bethlehem, because he was of the house and lineage of David, to be enrolled with Mary, his betrothed, who was with child. And while they were there, the time came for her to be delivered. And she gave birth to her first-born son and wrapped him in swaddling cloths, and laid him in a manger, because there was no place for them in the inn (Luke 2:4–7).

In sum, there is a major kind of biblical material which presents and appeals to historical events. The writers present those events as part of the information the reader is supposed to know. They appeal to those events as evidence for the larger claims they make about the nature of human life and the dealings of God with humankind. If it is appropriate to find out that Ulysses Grant was born in 1822 it seems equally appropriate to try to date, as closely as possible, when Absalom or Jesus was born. Almost no one today would deny that such historical questions can be brought to the biblical narratives and that such an historical enterprise is valid.

What is much more difficult and complicated is the question, what relationship do the historical details have to the authoritative claims of the Bible? Put differently, what difference does it make for faith whether our historical research confirms the specific claims of the Bible?

At least three things distinguish William McFeely's biography of Grant from the apparently historical material we see in 2 Samuel and Luke.

First, McFeely's fundamental purpose in telling the story of Ulysses Grant is to *tell* it, as accurately and interestingly as possible. His goal is to help the reader understand what happened as clearly as such understanding is possible.

What I found compelling about Grant as a subject for a biography was the man himself. I liked the way he looked; the picture of the mild, rather small person slouched comfortably in front of a tent suggested neither the fierce killing warrior nor the bumbling and perhaps crooked politician that I had often read about.[3]

The narrator tells the story of David in the Book of Samuel for reasons somewhat more complicated and mixed than that. To be sure he wishes to present something of the history of David's life and reign (there is no particular reason to suppose that the list of children presented in our passage is there for any reason other than to record accurate detail).

However, Gerhard von Rad catches something of the balance between straightforward history and interpretive point in the books of Samuel:

> The Succession Document is therefore in a very definite sense *theological* historiography. It is not a history of guidance in the ordinary sense, showing the hand of God directing everything for good, as the stories about Joseph, for example, do. Its subject is in fact a much more specific one—it deals with the anointed and his throne and so with the messianic problem[4] (italics mine).

Brevard Childs affirms the same theological focus for the books of Samuel:

> In the final shape of the book Nathan's promise to David in 2 Samuel 7 plays a crucial role for the composition as a whole. . . . The chapter takes up the theme of blessing but projects it into an eschatological, messianic promise. The blessings are "for ever" on the house of David (v. 29).[5]

The author of Luke-Acts is like the writer of the books of Samuel in that he, too, tries to present a story which is clear and valid according to the standards of the history writing of his time. He states his agenda in the literary dedication.

> Inasmuch as many have undertaken to compile a narrative of the things which have been accomplished among us, just as they were delivered to us by those who from the beginning were eyewitnesses and ministers of the word, it seemed good to me also, having followed all things closely for some time past, to write an orderly account for you, most excellent Theophilus, that you may know the truth concerning the things of which you have been informed. (Luke 1:1–4).

Yet theological studies of the Gospel of Luke make clear that the "truth" of which Luke wishes to inform Theophilus is not only, or even fundamentally factual truth: what happened when and who was there. What Luke wants to present is saving truth, truth which explains the activity of God in human history and evokes the appropriate response from human beings who are confronted with God's activity. God's activity centers and climaxes in the event of Jesus Christ.[6] Luke not only wishes to portray Jesus Christ as *a* figure in human history, but as *the* central figure in whom the meaning of history for human life is decisively disclosed. Moreover this Jesus whom he portrays represents the paradigmatic example of the faithful life for those who follow him and join the community he founds, the church.

Therefore while the fundamental concern of McFeely's work on Grant is to present the man as clearly as possible, the fundamental purposes of the books of Samuel and the Gospel of Luke move beyond that: they seek to persuade the reader not only of the truth about their central characters (David, Jesus) but to persuade the readers that God is particularly active in the histories of those protagonists; that in the history of David, God bestows blessing upon the people Israel; that in the history of Jesus, God bestows blessing upon all of humankind.

A second distinction between more contemporary histories like McFeely's *Grant* and the historical material in the Bible is closely related to the first distinction. It lies in the techniques the authors use. McFeely's concern is obviously to present his central figure as clearly and undogmatically as possible. The facts are ordered primarily to make the portrait clear and understandable. They are not ordered to persuade the reader to shift his or her fundamental apprehension of the nature of history, or the nature of God, or the purposes of human life.

Many scholars would suggest, however, that both the author of the books of Samuel and the author of Luke-Acts were concerned not only to present but to persuade, and that in the art of persuading they employed devices which may be understandable and valid for the preacher or the propagandist but which are not so appropriate for the historian.

Many scholars, for instance, think that at least part of the prophecy attributed to Nathan in 2 Sam. 7:4–16 represents a somewhat later interpretation of God's dealing with David and his offspring. It already presupposes the story of Solomon and the building of the temple and is written from the perspective of later generations of Judeans who find the promise for their blessing in the Davidic story.[7]

In Luke's brief account of the birth of Jesus other techniques appear. Is the claim that Jesus was born in Bethlehem an accurate historical report (as is apparently McFeely's report that Grant was born in Point Pleasant, Ohio)? Or might it be, as some have suggested, that the rather complicated story which moves Joseph and Mary from Nazareth to Bethlehem for Jesus' birth and then back to Nazareth again (cf. Luke 2:39) represents an attempt to show that Jesus is the expected Messiah of Israel, a Messiah who was prophesied in Mic. 5:2 to come from Bethlehem and was generally assumed to spring from the line of David? Another strain of tradition is evident in the Gospel of John (1:45) where it is assumed that Jesus derives from Nazareth, and where John's concern is not to insist that Jesus really came from Bethlehem but to insist that he really came from God (cf. John 7:25-31 and the argument about where Jesus comes from).

We assume that McFeely's account of Grant's birth is strictly accurate because we can find no reason in reading McFeely to suggest that he would have some special reason to interpret Grant's history rather oddly at this point, no reason to move Grant to his real birthplace, Georgetown, Ohio, only after describing his birth in his putative birthplace, Point Pleasant, Ohio. Luke (or the church before Luke) would have good reason for declaring that Jesus was born in Bethlehem rather than in Nazareth. To declare that Jesus was born in Bethlehem was one way of suggesting that Jesus was the one to whom the prophets pointed as the fulfillment of God's will.

This brings us to the third difference between McFeely's history and Luke-Acts (or 1—2 Samuel). In the understanding of Luke's story about Jesus or in understanding the Davidic history generally we have only the Christian documents themselves. We do not have any independent sources by which to check on their accuracy, and we can only make guesses about that accuracy by reference to occasional general secular information (like the silence in secular sources concerning the Roman census). We know that Luke used sources, because he tells us so, and we assume that 1 and 2 Samuel also represent the reworking of sources, but we don't know what those sources were and have no way of checking Luke's or the writer of Samuel's version against other material. In the case of McFeely's *Grant* we have one excellent source which he used, Grant's own *Memoirs* (again presumably accurate on the details of his birth since we can see no reason why he should choose not to be). For later details of Grant's life there is a wealth of other material: newspaper reports, memoirs of his contemporaries, and other accounts of his life and times which we can check against McFeely. It is therefore much harder for us to be certain about Luke's historical accuracy or that of the writer of 1 and 2 Samuel. We may have the intuitive sense that what they write of is the stuff of history (and the refusal to beautify the portrayal of King David, for instance, lends plausibility to our intuition), but we do not have the ways of testing their narrative that we have in the case of other, more recent "secular" historians.[8]

This description of the nature of "historical" narrative in the Bible raises a major problem for our understanding of the authority of this kind of biblical literature. Granted that the fundamental purpose of much of this material is to make a theological point—that God blesses Israel in the covenant with David, or that God redeems human history through the life, death, and resurrection of Jesus Christ—how far does the authority of that theological claim rest on the accuracy of the historical details? Is anything at stake for our faith in God, or our trust in the biblical witness, or our affirmation of God's particular relationship either to Israel or to Jesus of Nazareth if it turns out, for instance, that Jesus was born in Nazareth rather than in Bethlehem? Do we lose anything vital to our faith or to Scripture's authority if we find compelling evidence that Nathan's prophecy to David did not include the details of the reign of Solomon or the building of his temple?

Theologians have dealt with this problem in very nearly opposite ways.[9] Some theologians want to maintain that the Bible's authority is in large measure dependent on its accuracy as a presentation of history. Carl F. H. Henry speaks clearly for this "evangelical" perspective.

> Evangelical Christians maintain that the object of biblical faith can be historically investigated, at least to some extent. . . .
>
> Evangelical Christians repudiate the thesis shared by Barth, Brunner and Bultmann that divine revelation is never historically given and is therefore in no way historically investigatible. The dialectical-existential notion that disproof of the empty tomb would not at all affect the case for the resurrection of Jesus of Nazareth runs counter, evangelicals insist, to both New Testament teaching and its logic. Instead evangelical theists maintain that divine revelation is given in identifiable historical acts; moreover, a negative verdict concerning redemption history, if justified, would annul the credibility of Judeo-Christian religion.[10]

Henry does not claim that historical research can prove the validity of such central theological claims as God's unique revelation in Jesus of Nazareth, but he does seem to indicate that historical research might appropriately destroy faith and that larger interpretations of the patterns of history may help a person appropriate the faith.[11] That is to say that historical investigation is important for the establishment of faith, and in looking at texts like 2 Samuel or Luke it is important and appropriate to ask what really happened. The answer to that question is not a sufficient determinant of faith, but it is an important component of Christian faith.

On the other side, some writers have maintained that to ask the question "what really happened" is to mistake the nature of the biblical documents themselves. As I read Hans Frei's book *The Eclipse of Biblical Narrative*, there is, along with his analysis of the history of biblical interpretation, a claim about the reading of biblical narrative. Frei claims that it is a mistake to find the meaning or point of biblical narrative behind that narrative, whether in the history it purports to represent, or in the intention of its author, or in some other kind of meaning outside the text itself. The meaning of such realistic narratives as those we find in certain portions of Scripture (presumably including 2 Samuel and Luke) is to be found in the narrative itself: its characters, its plot, its shape.[12] That Frei's study so purports is suggested by his praise of Karl Barth in the preface:

> Barth distinguishes historical from realistic reading of the theologically most significant biblical narratives without falling into the trap of instantly making history the test of the *meaning* of the realistic form of the stories.[13]

Barth himself suggests that revelation, the core of the Bible's authority, is not dependent on historical observation and report.

> We should have once more to discard all that was previously said about the mystery in revelation, did we wish now to describe just a single one of the events of revelation narrated in the Bible as "historical," i.e., as apprehensible by a neutral observer or as apprehended by such a one. What the neutral observer of these events might apprehend or may have apprehended of these events was the form of the revelation, . . . but in no case revelation as such.[14]

Some theologians go further yet. Not only is faith in the biblical message independent of the historical accuracy of the Bible's narratives, to seek proof of such accuracy is itself detrimental to faith. True Christian faith needs to rely exclusively on the word and promises of God and should not be dependent on any kind of objective evidence. Faith should not rely on research of historians for its validation, nor should its confidence be threatened by their most radical findings. Faith which is genuine faith demands heartfelt trust and obedience, *not* the assent to claims based upon the results of historical research. Rudolf Bultmann maintains that the fact that Jesus was crucified is essential for Christian faith, but that beyond that "thatness" faith need not and must not depend upon historical information:

> It is the paradox of the Christian message that the eschatological event, according to Paul and John, is not to be understood as a dramatic cosmic catastrophe but as happening within history, beginning with the appearance of Jesus Christ and in continuity with this occurring again and again in history, but not as the kind of historical development which can be confirmed by any historian. It becomes an event repeatedly in preaching and faith. Jesus Christ is the eschatological event not as an established fact of past time but as repeatedly present, as addressing you and me here and now in preaching.[15]

Schubert Ogden, whose book *Christ Without Myth* interprets Bultmann and expands on his program, argues that reliance on historical inquiry can be a detriment to faith. Ogden argues thus with John Macquarrie:

> A second indication of the inadequacy of Macquarrie's position is his consistent affirmation that existential interpretation also needs to be "supplemented" by reference to a "minimum core of factuality," by which he means the person of the historical Jesus and, more particularly, Jesus' having actualized self-understanding. . . . But . . . the argument . . . seems to violate faith's own understanding of man before God. Is not the demand for such a "supplement" an implicit denial of man's radical freedom and responsibility and God's even more radical freedom and transcendence? Is it not, in short, a breach of the Reformation principles of *sola gratia—sola fide?*[16]

Since the purpose of this book is to understand the shape of biblical authority by an appeal to the biblical sources themselves, our response to the concerns of such theologians as Henry, Frei, Barth, and Bultmann must be based on our interpretation of the nature of the biblical narratives. I shall state briefly my reservations about each theologian's view and then seek a somewhat different understanding of the relation of history to authority in narrative portions of the Bible by a study of specific narrative material: the account of Jesus' crucifixion in two gospels.

Henry is careful not to insist that historical research is the fundamental grounds for faith. His claim that "divine revelation is given in identifiable historical acts," however, needs to be tempered by the reminder that what the historian can never identify is that the historical act is *revelatory.* The claim that what occurred not only happened according to the usual expectations of natural or historical causality and human decision but also happened according to the plan and mercy of God is not a claim that the most careful attention to the facts could ever affirm. In Henry's paradigmatic case, the empty tomb, even if the most exhaustive historical research could establish that shortly after Jesus' burial his tomb was found empty, that fact would be subject to a variety of interpretations. The Gospel of Matthew, which assumes the fact of the empty tomb, recognizes the possibility of such varied interpretations by seeking to refute the charge that the tomb was empty because Jesus' disciples had stolen the body (cf. Matt. 28:13). To many Christians it is equally the case that should the story of the empty tomb be conclusively *disproven,* what they take to be fundamental about the resurrection faith would not be affected.

It is clear even for Matthew, for whom the story of the empty tomb was part of the recitation of the "saving events" of Jesus' story, that that event must be interpreted in a much larger and richer framework. Within that framework the one who had been in the tomb not only is no longer there; he has been raised by God, given that authority which hitherto had been reserved for God alone, vindicated as the true teacher not only of Israel but of the Gentiles, and established as the living Lord, present to the ongoing experience of the church. No historical evidence could sufficiently sustain such claims. Certainly proof of the accuracy of the accounts of an empty tomb would not do so.

Frei seems to reduce all of biblical narrative to one essential form: the realistic or history-like tale. However, our brief description of the canonical material indicates that the diversity of narrative is much richer than that. While, as Frei suggest, it may be inappropriate to try to look behind the story of the binding of Isaac for some meaning located in external history, such narratives as the succession material in Samuel and Kings and the Gospel of Luke, which deliberately locates Jesus' story in the reign of particular emperors and specific governors, push the reader of the narrative behind the narrative to some understanding of that history which it relates. To say that Scripture is rich with parable is not to say that every story contained therein should be read parabolically.

Barth (at least in some of the modes of his many-faceted theology), Bultmann, and Ogden, while rightly trying to protect faith from undue reliance on the latest findings or guesses by historical critics, nonetheless run the risk of removing redemption from the realm of real history and locating God's activity in something outside a tangible incarnation. George Stroup characterizes the theological problem:

> From the beginning the Christian community has insisted that the incarnation of God's Word in Jesus of Nazareth means that salvation is an utterly concrete, tangible, earthy reality that takes place in the particularity of one person's narrative history. . . . When Christians talk about redemption, what is redeemed is not just the human soul, but the whole person and that means human history.[17]

Nils Dahl draws the appropriate conclusions for historical criticism:

> That faith is relatively uninterested in the historical Jesus research does not mean that it is absolutely uninterested in it. To draw this conclusion would be a kerygmatic theological Docetism, or even a denial of faith in God as Creator, under whose worldly rule even the historian does his service as a scholar. The fact that Jesus can be made an object of historical critical research is given with the incarnation and cannot be denied by faith, if the latter is to remain true to itself.[18]

Frei seems to alter the fundamental Christian proclamation that the Word became flesh to the claim that the Word became narrative. Bultmann tends toward the affirmation that the Word continually becomes proclamation.

While each theologian points to an essential aspect of biblical literature (its narrative form, its use as a source for preaching) each leaves out or underestimates the peculiar possibilities and difficulties posed by the essential claim that the Christian narrative narrates the history of a real man, and that Christian preaching proclaims the significance of a life lived within the limitations of genuine historical existence.

JESUS' CRUCIFIXION

In order better to understand the nature of "historical" narrative in the Bible itself, we can examine two different narrative presentations of an event which is held by virtually all Christians to be central to the understanding of faith, the event of Jesus' crucifixion. A comparison between the crucifixion narrative in the Gospel of Mark and the crucifixion narrative in the Gospel of Luke may help us to understand how history and faith come together in biblical narratives.

Most scholars would agree that *Mark's Gospel* provides us with the earliest narrative account of Jesus' crucifixion (Mark 15:21–39). What seem to be the historical "facts" of this description, and where does interpretation enter in? We shall see that that question of interpretation is easier to answer in the case of Luke's account, since we assume he is interpreting Mark, but even in the case of Mark some suggestions seem plausible.

We already saw, in comparing Jesus' birth story to McFeely's account of the birth of U.S. Grant, that the early church was concerned to show that the shape of Jesus' life fit a pattern which could be derived from an attentive reading of the Old Testament. There, we suspected, the concern to show that Jesus was born in Bethlehem derived in part from attention to the claims of the prophet Micah, who predicted the rule of Israel would come from David's city (Mic. 5:2). Here the account of Jesus' crucifixion is strongly reminiscent, in some of its features, of Psalm 22.

> My God, my God, why hast thou forsaken me?
> Why art thou so far from helping me, from the words
> of my groaning?
> All who see me mock at me,
> they make mouths at me, they wag their heads;
> "He committed his cause to the LORD, let him deliver him,
> let him rescue him, for he delights in him!"
> they divide my garments among them,
> and for my raiment they cast lots (Ps. 22:1, 7–8, 18).

It we assume that Psalm 22 was not originally a prophetic psalm whose details were wondrously fulfilled in Jesus' crucifixion (cf. note 7 above), then it seems likely that Mark or the early church has shaped the story they tell in the light of the Old Testament passage. The great scandal which the early church had to proclaim and transcend was the scandal that the one it declared to be Messiah and Son of God had been crucified as an outlaw. One way to overcome something of the embarrassment of that claim was to suggest that Jesus' death took place as part of God's overarching plan for humankind. The place to look for God's overarching plan was in Scripture, in what Christians call the Old Testament. Rightly read, Scripture revealed that Jesus' crucifixion, far from denying the power of God, confirmed what God had intended for humankind from the start.

In comparing the narrative of Davidic kingship or the Lukan portrayal of Jesus' birth with the description of Grant in McFeely's biography, we further suggested that the author of 1 and 2 Samuel and the evangelist Luke both wanted to do more than present their stories as clearly as possible. They used literary devices to persuade the readers of the fundamental, ongoing significance of their stories for the life of those who read the stories with faith.

In Mark's account of the crucifixion we can also see those devices which seem to point us beyond the story to its ongoing significance. One of the major concerns of Mark's Gospel is to insist that the good news of what God has done in Jesus Christ is good news not only for Jews but for the Gentiles. Therefore it is quite appropriate to Mark's theological concerns that he should relate the story of the sundering of the temple curtain. The curtain was a sign of the particular presence of God within the sanctuary in Jerusalem. With the splitting of the curtain, God's presence is made accessible to the larger, Gentile world.

So, too, it is significant that the only human figure in the gospel who affirms Mark's central message—that Jesus is Son of God—is a Gentile, the Roman centurion: "Truly this man was the Son of God" (15:39). Whatever the various figures at the foot of the cross may have said "in fact," there is certainly good reason in Mark's larger theological purpose for his telling of a Gentile person who came to faith at the foot of the cross.

Whatever truth may lie behind the claim of the opposition of Jewish leaders to Jesus' ministry, the remark of the chief priests and scribes, "He saved others; he cannot save himself" (15:31), now represents an ironic interpretation of the whole scene. For all the wrong reasons, the priests and scribes say exactly the right thing: Jesus cannot save himself if he is to save others. By his refusal to save himself he becomes savior to humankind.

In all these ways, surely, Mark is not content to present an account of "what actually happened," assuming that he had any access to such an account. He rather stresses the fact that what actually happened had its origins in the ongoing purposes of God and its outcome in the enrichment and redemption of the lives of humankind.

Other features of the story seem less easily explicable as part of Mark's theological program. They have a touch of the irrefractable; they suggest the stuff of more narrowly defined historical fact.

One such instance is the reference to Simon of Cyrene, bolstered by the comment that he was the father of Alexander and Rufus. We might suspect that the readers know Alexander and Rufus, and that this is a friendly reference to the relationship of familiar figures to the story Mark recites.

Another piece of likely historical evidence is the accusation made against Jesus that he claimed he would destroy the temple. The connection between Jesus' crucifixion and a threat to the temple is made several times in the gospel tradition (cf. Matt. 26:57–63, John 2:19–22, Acts 6:14), but always tends to be interpreted away or underplayed. It seems to have no special theological significance but it rather seems to be something of an embarrassment. When something does not fit the gospels' theology so well, it often has stronger claims to being a clue to a missing piece of history.

It is much harder to make a judgment about the historicity of Jesus' cry: "My God, my God, why hast thou forsaken me?" (Mark 15:34). On the one hand, as we have already seen, Mark shapes his account of the Passion Narrative with details drawn in large part from Psalm 22, and Jesus' cry consists of the first line of that psalm. On the other hand, Luke—who apparently had Mark's Gospel before him—may have found that cry an embarrassment and so reinterpreted Jesus' last word as the more acceptable, "Into thy hands I commit my spirit" (Luke 23:46). Either we have a reminiscence which Mark preserved and Luke omitted, or we have a radical interpretation by Mark himself of the significance of the crucifixion, an interpretation which suggests that Jesus' sonship is recognized precisely in his moment of abandonment and that God's moment of redemption occurs just at the point where Jesus feels most rejected by God. The theological puzzle is this: does the power of the story to depict redemption in the midst of abandonment depend on its historical accuracy? If Jesus' last words are in fact forever lost and the cry of dereliction represents Mark's interpretation of the story, does that detract from the power of the story to represent both the scandal and the comfort of the cross?

Apart from this particularly puzzling problem, we can say some things fairly clearly about Mark's account of the passion. The fact that Jesus was crucified could be doubted only by the most athletic skepticism. However, were historical scholarship somehow to disprove that datum, it seems unlikely that Mark's story could persuasively claim to display the dealing of God with humankind in the life and death of the man Jesus.

The other accurate historical details are interesting but seem to avail little for the significance of the story for Christian faith. That Simon is the name of the man who carried the cross and that he had sons (Rufus and Alexander), that Jesus was charged with threatening to destroy the temple, that the charge brought against him had to do with claims to be the King of the Jews—all help us understand something of the original historical context, but the details *do not* move us toward the point of the story.

The richer interpretive devices are more likely devices—the ironic christological claim of the priests; the setting of the story in the context of an older text, Psalm 22; the veil in the temple rent in two; a Gentile finding faith at the foot of the cross. I doubt that these happened exactly as described. I doubt that they need to have happened exactly as described. They do what they are supposed to do: they move the narrative beyond Golgotha and the small circle there to a larger world and a larger circle who need to know that the story is a story told for them, and that what *did* happen on Golgotha happened for them and their salvation.

If this is a story about God's activity in human history, then in Mark's context the claim that God has acted means two things: First, this is a story which looks back to other stories which have had power to reveal. Here Psalm 22 provides that background which moves the story of Golgotha back from its present to the deeper and darker mysteries of God. Second, this is a story which looks forward to embrace later readers, later listeners. It is a story which must declare the events in such a way that other generations can be enticed to rethink their own lives and their own possibilities in the light of the event which is told.

In the case of Jesus' crucifixion, the telling of the narrative would not have the power it has could we not also say with confidence: it *did* happen to that man, in that place, on a real cross. But it would also not have the power it has apart from Mark's rooting it in a long antecedent history of claims about the meaning and purposes of God. And it would not have the power it has apart from those devices which use such characters as unbelieving priests and believing centurions to expand the picture toward a wider audience and a future so far only guessed.

In *Luke's Gospel* account of Jesus' crucifixion, we can see the ways in which theological interpretation shapes "historical" narrative even more clearly. It is reasonably clear that Luke's primary source for his story of the crucifixion is Mark. For the most part the details he adds or the changes he makes do not represent special historical information which he possessed and used to correct the Markan account. For the most part these changes represent Luke's special theological emphases used to interpret his source (Luke 23:26–49).

In his interpretation of the crucifixion, Luke—like Mark—places the event within the context of the ongoing purposes of God by linking what happens fairly closely to the fulfillment of Scripture. Again details from Psalm 22 (in the dividing of the garments, Luke 23:34, Ps. 22:18) and Psalm 69 (the vinegar, Luke 23:36, Ps. 69:21) suggest a background in God's plan for Jesus' crucifixion. That background is revealed in Scripture. Furthermore, Luke omits Jesus' cry of abandonment and substitutes instead a quotation from Psalm 31 as Jesus' final cry: "Into thy hands I commit my spirit" (Luke 23:46; Ps. 31:5, Masoretic Text, Ps. 31:6). Again the scandal of the crucifixion is illumined, if not lessened, by the claim that a right reading of God's intention revealed through the psalms would indicate that the crucifixion should rightly be read as part of God's plan.

In at least three ways Luke also makes clear the way in which the story of the crucifixion has significance for the history which follows it, how it reaches out to embrace the present needs and concerns of Luke's readers.

Luke 23:28–31 is almost certainly a Lukan addition to the passion story. It relates the crucifixion of Jesus to the larger history of the people of Judea and suggests that the fall of the city and the destruction of the temple (which probably antedated the writing of Luke's gospel) were part of God's judgment for Jesus' crucifixion. So the event of the crucifixion has continuing effect in history: it explains an event in Luke's recent past (the fall of Jerusalem), and it suggests the ongoing presence of God in history, doing justice and revealing truth through historical events.

The story of the two thieves in Luke 23:39–43 also represents a Lukan interpretation of the meaning of Jesus' death, whatever core of historical reminiscence may lie behind it. As the warning to the daughters of Jerusalem suggests something of the ongoing significance of the crucifixion for the history of cities and nations, the story of the two thieves suggests something of the significance of the crucifixion for the lives of individuals. The two thieves represent erring humankind faced with a decision before the cross of Jesus. The unbelieving thief seeks only the kind of miracle which would vitiate the whole point of God's redemptive act in the cross. Jesus is to save himself and rescue the thieves. The believing thief sees more clearly the significance of the crucifixion of the man beside him. Jesus is the one who dies innocently while others die in guilt. Because of his innocence Jesus is the one who, by his dying, provides access to the kingdom of God. The story of the two thieves becomes an example for future readers, pondering the odd story of the cross, wondering whether it is a story of a man's failure or of God's successful redemption of humankind, and having to decide whether or not to have faith in the cross as redemptive.

The changes which Luke makes in the very close of the story in part reflect his uneasiness with the starkness of Mark's depiction of the crucifixion. Now Jesus no longer asks, "My God, my God, why hast thou forsaken me?" but says instead, "Father, into thy hands I commit my spirit" (Luke 23:46). The centurion no longer takes Christ's abandonment as a sign of his sonship, but hearing the cry of resignation declares, "Certainly this man was innocent" (23:47). More than that, however, Luke's ending of the story represents a further claim about the ongoing significance of Jesus' crucifixion. Jesus here becomes an example for the church which is to succeed him, and especially for those who are called upon to be martyrs for their faith. Just as Jesus in all innocence is martyred and yet entrusts his spirit to God, so succeeding generations of faithful Christians are to commend their spirits to God when faced with persecution and even death.

We can see Luke's understanding of the relationship between Jesus' death and that of later martyrs in his portrayal of the martyrdom of Stephen in the book of Acts, the second part of his two-volume history of Jesus and the church. In Acts 7:59, just before his death, Stephen echoes Jesus' last words and prays, "Lord Jesus, receive my spirit," and echoing Jesus' prayer for forgiveness, he adds: "Lord, do not hold this sin against them" (7:60).

Therefore in Luke's gospel we can see quite clearly that though Luke starts with a source which gives an account of Jesus' death (Mark's gospel), he is quite willing to move beyond the presentation of that source to interpret its significance, to show the ways in which the deed of the cross also represents the activity of God. Again Luke does this in two different ways. First, he suggests that the background for the event lies in God's providential plan for humankind and that the evidence for that providential plan is to be found in the Old Testament. Second, he suggests that the consequences of the event claim the attention, understanding, and decision of his own readers and of the generations to follow. Rightly to understand the crucifixion is to understand the way in which God works judgment in history. Rightly to perceive the crucifixion is to perceive that the reader is called to a decision whether Jesus' death represents ultimate weakness or God's redemptive power for believers. Rightly to appropriate the crucifixion is to be ready for faithful martyrdom according to the example of Jesus, should that martyrdom be the lot of the believer.

We are now able in summary fashion to use the crucifixion accounts of

Mark and Luke to make some suggestions about the ways in which historical narrative works in the Bible and some clues for the ways in which it may be authoritative today.

First, it is clear that behind these narratives lie some virtually irrefutable facts and that part of the ongoing authority and power of the narrative lies in the claim that they refer to actual historical event. It seems fairly clear that the claims which Mark and Luke wish to draw about the significance of Jesus' crucifixion, as the fulfillment of the Old Testament and the sign of God's dealing with humankind, depend on God's *actually* having dealt with humankind on Golgotha. If the story is only illustrative it becomes unclear what it illustrates, or whom it represents. It cannot be only a story of how God *might* deal with humankind should God ever choose to do so. More than that it may be that something of the shape of the narrative itself needs to correspond to the "facts" in order for the accounts to represent God's redemptive activity as they claim to do. It is not clear that we could rightly read the story as a sign of God's activity for us in Jesus Christ if we learned that Jesus died because he was a malefactor or a wicked and deceitful man. Nor is it clear that the story would have the same power to shape and illumine the lives of the readers could we be sure that Jesus went to the cross protesting to the last, desperately begging those who convicted him to change their minds and set him free.

Yet the facts, even could we get them all, would hardly tell the tale. The most historical evidence one could probably ever gain is the account of a man executed by Roman authorities for offenses which did not violate the fundamental integrity of his life. What the facts cannot yield are the richer adumbrations which both gospel accounts present as integral to the story they wish to tell. What the interpreter sees in the story and helps us to see in retelling the story is a richer context which makes the story Scripture and not simply interesting reminiscence.

The richer context includes the presentation of that background which places the story in an ongoing pattern of events which the gospel writers claim were saving events, which places the story within the pattern of God's purposes. This background is presented largely by reference to Scripture, to older traditions already seen as authoritative accounts of God and God's will. The richer context also includes the suggestion of those implications which the story continues to have, so that its effect is lived out in the ongoing history of individual believers, of the church, and of humankind.[19] Rightly to read the story is to know that the God who is purported to act therein is still present, calling for decision, doing judgment, inspiring faithfulness, comforting fears. In the oddest and strongest claim of Mark's gospel, rightly to read the story is to perceive that God is sometimes most present in the experience of the absence of God.

What we have said of the New Testament crucifixion passages could be multiplied for other gospel narratives and for Old Testament narratives as well. The story of the exodus is enriched by being placed within a background (God's promises to Abraham, Isaac, and Jacob) and by casting its shadow forward (on the exile and its pain; on the celebration of the passover meal). The story of David is given historical background in God's failed attempt to use judges to rule Israel, and stands over the generations of kings which follow David as both a judgment and a promise. Historical narrative in the Bible never narrowly describes the time of the events portrayed. Historical narrative in the Bible suggests those preparations which preceded the story and those implications which shall emerge from it. Because Scripture maintains that the past reveals God's purpose and the future will present God's demands for human decision, that link which biblical narrative makes between past and future is a part of what we mean when we claim that biblical narrative portrays, not only human history, but the activity of God.

DEALING WITH HISTORICAL NARRATIVE TODAY

This brings us then to the final question. If the authority of historical narrative in Scripture rests both in the facts and in their interpretation, both in the tale told and in its links to a past and a future, how can those narratives be used authoritatively in contemporary Christian reflection and practice?

BIBLICAL NARRATIVE AND HISTORICAL RESEARCH

It is clear by now that historical research in itself is insufficient for the validation of scriptural authority. No fundamental claim which biblical narrative makes can be confirmed by the findings of historical research alone.

On the other hand, the richer interpretive claims which Scripture makes about the history which it recites cannot be totally divorced from that history, either. Different Christians will make different decisions about what evidence is more or less crucial to the faith. For some, like Henry, for instance, the reliability of the account of the empty tomb is essential (cf. above, p. 48). For other Christians the accuracy of that account makes little difference in their own interpretation of Christ's history and its significance for contemporary believers. We have suggested that for us and for many Christians the fact of Jesus' crucifixion and of his integrity is essential to the authority of the Christian story, though it should be clear by now that even if the claim that Jesus died an innocent man in a ghastly way is absolutely established historically, that claim in itself will not provide the full implications which Christian writers like Mark and Luke wish to draw. It is a given, however, with the historical basis of some biblical material, that part of the way to establish and understand the authority of Scripture is to apply to its narratives the test of historical research.

Furthermore, if it is true that biblical narrative always makes claims more complicated than simply the claim to historicity, our understanding of those more complex interpretive claims may also be enriched by attention to historical research. In understanding Luke's interpretation of the crucifixion it *does* help to know that Mark was probably one source for Luke's gospel, and the information that Luke used Mark is information derived from certain kinds of historical and literary analysis. Insofar as we can reconstruct (somewhat independently) the story of the Kings of Israel and Judah who succeeded Solomon, we can understand the extent to which the biblical writers have reshaped their histories around fundamental theological concerns: did the Kings encourage or not encourage the worship of the Baalim?

Even if we choose to attend to the narrative more closely than to the history behind it, our interpretation of the narrative sometimes demands some hypotheses concerning the history. The authority of biblical "historical" narrative can never depend entirely on historical research, but neither can it be divorced entirely from such research.

THE ADUMBRATION OF THE STORY: INTERPRETATION

I have claimed that the richness of the biblical historical narratives is suggested by the writers in two directions. On the one hand the narratives are placed in the context of the tradition of God's dealing with humankind. On the other hand the narratives are extended forward by suggesting their implications for the life of their readers and of the generations to come.

The contemporary reader can find the authority of the biblical tale in part by trying to place himself or herself in the context of those first readers—Mark's community, or Luke's community, or the people in exile wishing to return to Jerusalem and to a good Davidic king. Imaginatively we can sense something of the ways in which the story reaches back to embrace a past which was the past of its first readers; we can sense the ways in which it reaches out to suggest implications for the present situation in which they lived.

Yet more than that, there are ways in which these narratives now become, for contemporary Christians, something of that background out of which we read and understand our lives. In the story of the crucifixion it is not only the psalms which for us provide tradition, a tradition adumbrating the purposes of God. The account of Jesus' crucifixion (whatever else it does) also provides something of that tradition. More than that, what for the initial readers were present implications (God's activity in the fall of Jerusalem; God's promise to first-century Christian martyrs) have for us *also* become largely background. The first readers' present and immediate future are to us past: they provide the context out of which we must interpret our own present. Nor only the psalms but Golgotha and the persecution of the Lukan church cast their shadow over the present in which we live and the future for which we must decide.

Therefore, since we maintain that the past these stories adumbrate is God's past, it is bad faith simply to assume that those ancient narratives no longer help us know ourselves or choose our future. On the other hand, since the gospel writers always used narrative and tradition to point ahead, it is equally bad faith to assume that we stand precisely where Luke's community stood, or that we dwell in exile in Babylon waiting for a new Davidic king. Out of those earlier situations we derive the material to interpret our own somewhat different present.

To the extent that the biblical history (with its background and its implications) provides the context for our own history, the appropriation of the authority of biblical narrative requires at least three stages.

First, contemporary Christians wish to attend to the setting of the original narrative in its historical context as closely and intelligently as possible. What did happen on Golgotha or in Jerusalem between David and the prophet of the Lord? What earlier tradition helped interpret those events for those who read the narratives? How were those events interpreted for those early readers?

Second, contemporary Christians wish to attend to the shape of their own lives, that of their communities, that of the history in which they live. Luke perceived patterns in his history: patterns of judgment, of belief and unbelief, of martyrdom. What patterns emerge as we observe ourselves and our communities?

Third, contemporary Christians seek to find the imaginative (and faithful) connections between those formative narratives and our present situation. Where are there correspondences, differences? Where does the older narrative help us see the pattern in present events? (Surely Luke was helped to perceive the nature of judgment in his time by his reading of the crucifixion events. He saw the pattern in part because he knew the story.)

In this way contemporary Christians stand somewhat where Mark and Luke and the author of 1 and 2 Samuel stood. There is a history behind us which our ancestors have claimed is the history of God's acts. If indeed God acted in that history, we may be sure that that history has continuing implications for *our* history. Faithfully to claim its authority is faithfully and imaginatively to seek the ways in which the lineaments of the past provide the clues to the present and the opportunities for the future. Authority rests not in the simple repetition of the biblical narrative but in its appropriation.

THE RE-ENACTMENT OF THE STORY: RITUAL AND SACRAMENT

Because the communities of Israel and the church believed that the narratives they told represented the activity of God, they believed that those narratives had ongoing implications for the lives of those who told and heard them.

The belief in the ongoing power of the narrative was evidenced not only in the willingness to interpret and re-interpret narrative, but also in the ongoing re-enactment of the central narratives of the believing communities. For the people of Israel the great festivals of their faith largely represented re-enactments and reappropriations of their central historical narratives.

Popular Christianity has sometimes been more open than more academic theologies to the power of the simple re-enactment of the story. Hymns and spirituals simply assume that in retelling the narrative the congregation is allowed to re-enact the formative events: "Were you there when they crucified my Lord?" "Go down, Moses, go way down in Egypt's land; tell old Pharoah, let my people go," "O sacred head now wounded."

Our earliest source for the practice of the early church, the letters of Paul, makes clear that for the church the fundamental events of the narrative of Jesus, the story of the Last Supper and of Jesus' crucifixion and resurrection, are not only the subject of Christian reflection or interpretation, but are themselves re-enacted and reappropriated in the Lord's supper and baptism.

> For as often as you eat this bread and drink the cup, you proclaim the Lord's death until he comes (1 Cor. 11:26).

Do you not know that all of us who have been baptized into Christ Jesus were baptized into his death? We were buried therefore with him by baptism into death, so that as Christ was raised from the dead by the glory of the Father, we too might walk in newness of life (Rom. 6:3–4).

Through festival, ritual, and sacrament "time past and time future . . . point to one end, which is always present."[20] Last Supper, crucifixion, burial, and resurrection are no longer the background for our faith—the traditions to be interpreted. In sacrament they become again the central events of God's acting: foreshadowed by the past, casting their shadow upon the future, caught up in a present which faith understands as God's present.

RESURRECTION AND HISTORY

Finally, the right appeal of Christian faith to the authority of its narrative history can never be confused with the assumption that God will do precisely as God has always done. The fundamental pattern at the heart of history, as Christians understand it, is resurrection, and the heart of resurrection is surprise. Rightly to read the narratives and to interpret our own history in the light of the narratives is to realize that every day, expectations may be reversed, patterns shifted, and God may open the present to a future which seems astonishingly new.

"FICTIONAL" NARRATIVE IN THE BIBLE

Some narrative material in the Bible makes neither explicit nor implicit claim to provide historical information. Rightly to read or to hear these narratives is to know that they present themselves as stories.

The earliest gospel, Mark, introduces the tale of the sower and the other stories of Mark 4 by the explicit claim, "And he taught them many things in parables," that is, in stories (cf. 4:2). The introductions to the parables, which refer simply to unnamed sowers, or travelers, or fathers, give us the clue that what we have here is not a report of an actual event, but a fiction told with a specific purpose.

"Listen! A sower went out to sow . . ." (Mark 4:3).
"A man was going down from Jerusalem to Jericho . . ." (Luke 10:30).
"There was a man who had two sons . . ." (Luke 15:11).

These introductions indicate that what is to follow is a good story, just as clearly as the traditional beginning of a children's tale, "Once upon a time," tells us that a story is about to begin.

It would be just as inappropriate to ask, "Where was the sower's field?" or "What was the name of the traveler to Jericho?" or "Just exactly how old were the two sons?" as it would be to ask, "Once upon *what* time? Be more specific." The purpose of the parable is not to convey historical information but to do something else entirely.

So, too, there are Old Testament narratives which have the clear ring of fiction. The Book of Job begins as a good story might well do:

> There was a man in the land of Uz, whose name was Job; and that man was blameless and upright, one who feared God, and turned away from evil (Job 1:1).

Uz is as fictional a land as Oz, and Job himself a creation of a storyteller (a creation whose story becomes a significant story for readers from the first reading until now). The point of the story does not rest in our ability to reconstruct the history which lies behind it.[21]

Other Old Testament literature, too, is almost certainly to be read as significant fiction without attention to questions of historical accuracy: the first eleven chapters of Genesis, the story of Jonah and the great fish, the accounts of Daniel and his confrontations with Nebuchadnezzar, are among the materials almost certainly to be understood as revealing fictions rather than historical accounts.

In all of these cases the question of the relationship of faith to history or interpretation to history, therefore, does not arise. The question is rather, what kind of authority can a story have for the faith and life of the contemporary Christian or the contemporary church.

THE PARABLES

From the earliest days of Christianity it has been clear that the parables had some point beyond the telling of a good story, and Christians have sought to discover and to proclaim that point.

As early as the Gospels themselves, we have evidence that the early church felt that it was not enough simply to repeat a parable; it was essential to interpret that parable for the listeners or the readers. So, for instance, Mark 4:3–8 tells the parable of the sower, quite probably in much the same form that Jesus originally told it. However, some early Christian interpreter has added to the original story a rather elaborate explanation in Mark 4:14–20. The explanation uses language which seems to be derived not from Jesus, but from the early church. Its explanation is itself a bit confused (at first the seed represents the "word" and then it represents different sorts of believers). Many scholars have argued, therefore, that the interpretation is separable from the parable and is in fact a later attempt to try to explain the "meaning" of the story.[22]

For centuries allegory was apparently used as a major device for interpreting the parables: each feature of the parable could be seen as a cryptic sign for some religious truth which lay outside the parable itself.[23]

Among biblical critics, the scholar who delivered the understanding of Jesus' parables from the domination of the allegorical method was Adolf Jülicher. Jülicher argued that not only the church fathers but also the gospel-writers before them were mistaken in trying to give an interpretation for each feature of the parable.[24] On the contrary, Jülicher argues, in Jesus' own preaching the parables were not puzzles to be solved by the ingenuity of interpreters. They were illustrations of abiding spiritual truth.

Where Jülicher differed from later interpreters of parables who built on his work—C. H. Dodd and Joachim Jeremias—was that he usually thought the point of the parable was a broadly applicable moral principle: the broader the application, the more likely it was to be a correct interpretation of the parable itself.[25]

Dodd and Jeremias sought to do more thoroughly what Jülicher had first attempted: to interpret the parables in their original setting in the teaching of Jesus. For Dodd the fundamental framework for understanding Jesus' parables was not a framework of general moral principles but Jesus' specific preaching of the presence of the kingdom among those who heard him. Jeremias, too, thought that the motif of the kingdom was central to Jesus' parables and thought more specifically that the original context for the telling of the parables was usually a dispute between Jesus and his opponents or a remark to the crowd. Both scholars sought to cut through the accretions which the early church and the evangelists had added to the parables in order to come close to the words of Jesus himself.[26]

Both Dodd and Jeremias, however, continued to assume, as Jülicher had argued, that each parable has *a* fundamental point. Further, each saw his work as trying to interpret that fundamental point in the light of the ministry and preaching of Jesus.

Later scholars have had difficulty with the assumption that we can best interpret parables by explaining them, by paraphrasing them, by saying what they "really mean."[27] What follows is my own interpretation of the recent history of parable interpretation and my own attempt to suggest somewhat richer ways of interpreting parables than by the attempt to paraphrase. Rather diverse in itself, parable scholarship often discusses the ways in which parable criticism needs to be more sensitive to the parable as a kind of literature, a story or an extended metaphor. I draw on these works but do not identify myself entirely with any one of them.

Recent literary criticism has suggested that a piece of literature which has integrity and which shows imaginative power (for instance, a fine poem) cannot simply be translated into another form of discourse (for instance, a prose "explanation"). Even the simplest metaphor derives its power in part from the fact that what it says cannot be said in any other way.

W. H. Auden writes:

"In the deserts of the heart,
Let the healing fountain start."[28]

We can make some sense of the metaphors by contrasting deserts to fountains by suggesting reasons Auden might have thought that hearts were particularly barren when he wrote this poem (1939) and by setting these verses in the context of the larger tribute to W. B. Yeats. But none of this will substitute for the thing itself. It will not do to read our explanation of the poem and think that we have a worthy substitute for the poetry.

So, too, with that most familiar line of Hebrew poetry, "The Lord is my shepherd" (Ps. 23:1). The line can be interpreted and explained, the nature of shepherding in ancient Palestine discussed, the line related to the rest of the psalm which follows, general doctrines on the sovereignty and care of God extrapolated. But none of these will be the line, the metaphor. The line is not to be confused with its explanations; it is richer than they. Were it not richer then they, we could substitute the explanations for Psalm 23 in the Bible and in the liturgy of the church.

So, too, I would suggest as many others have, that the parable has power precisely because it *is* parable. Like a good metaphor or a good poem it defies precise definition or adequate translation. One can get *at* its meaning by interpretation, but one cannot *get* its meaning.

More than that, a parable is not only a metaphor, it is a story. And like a good story or a good play, it not only conveys information to the reader or listener, it acts upon the reader or listener in ways that are more subtle than information. Traditionally the most powerful dramas or stories are those which bring the viewer, the hearer, into their world. They provide not so much new facts as new horizons. The audience goes away not so much with new knowledge as with new wisdom, new perspective, perhaps new sympathies. On one level the story of Hamlet is stated simply: A man sets out to revenge the murder of his father by his uncle-stepfather and encounters certain obstacles along the way. One can buy a plot synopsis and find out who kills whom in the last scene of the last act. But the plot synopsis is not the play because it does not bring the audience into the murky world of Elsinore, confront the audience with that array of decisions and indecisions which Hamlet enacts, and finally move the audience to a broader sympathy, not only for the plight of the populace of Elsinore, but perhaps for the pains and possibilities of that larger world which Elsinore enables us to see anew. Parables are more like plays than they are like propositions. They involve us, shift us, challenge us, illumine us, and at best enrich the resources of our emotions.

To read the story of the Prodigal son (Luke 15:11–32) and his brother *as* story is to see that what it provides is not precisely either a moral lesson or a sermon illustration. What is presented is rather more a shift of one's horizons, a challenge to one's expectations, a question.

Note, however, a few devices of the parable. For one thing the parable remains unresolved. The conclusion sets the fundamental question to the elder brother and to the listener: "Will you join in the celebration for your prodigal brother returned?" No answer is given; we do not know what the older brother decides, and are left to decide for ourselves, or challenged to decide for ourselves.

Furthermore, the parable not only refuses to make one point but also refuses to speak from one perspective. Whether we are more inclined to think of ourselves as prodigals or as older brothers, the device of the story is a clever one. The story of the Prodigal son is told in such simple, moving detail that it is impossible not to sympathize with him when he comes to himself, or to rejoice with him when he sees his father running, all dignity discarded, down the road. Yet just where we are most content to rest in the happy ending we are reminded that other issues remain, and there is another perspective on this story. The younger son does not get all the good lines. The elder brother's grievance is a just one, and the story gives the grievance its due.

The father is like God, but not exactly identified with God. When the son comes home he says that he has sinned both before his heavenly father and before his earthly one. The father is caught with a dilemma, too. How can he be father to the prodigal without betraying the loyalty of the one who stayed at home? Twice the father goes out to greet a son, one on the way home from the far country, one on the way home from the fields.

No single perspective tells the story, and the listener is not allowed to remain content with any single version of the story's meaning. The reader is not only left with a question, but is questioned: "Where do you fit here? And if you fit more places than one, what does that mean?"

Parables involve the devices which involve us, and the shifts of perspective and refusals of resolution which question us. They cannot be translated into non-story form because it is precisely the story which can involve us so as to shift our understandings of ourselves, our world, and God. It may not even be the case at the end of a parable that we can describe precisely what we see differently but only that we can acknowledge *that* we see differently, or intend to act differently, or to hope more confidently.

Finally, fairness to the story form of the parables requires attention to the fact that Jesus' parables are always presented as part of larger stories, the gospels. In the case of the parable of the Prodigal son, for instance, Luke helps us to interpret the parable by placing it in juxtaposition with two other parables where someone rejoices over the discovery of a precious good which has been lost: the sheep in Luke 15:4–7 and the coin in Luke 15:8–10. Further, the whole complex of parables is placed within the story of the ministry of Jesus, who in Luke's Gospel especially is presented as one who seeks the lost for the sake of God's kingdom. Reading the story of the prodigal in the light of Luke's gospel we can say not only that the story helps us to become aware of the ways in which God runs out to welcome the lost who return home, we can suggest that God turns to the lost precisely in Jesus Christ, the one who tells the parable. The parable by itself, of course, does not make this connection, but since we read the parable in the context of the larger story, to apply the parable to the ministry of Jesus is to recognize one appropriate nuance of its significance.

LONGER NARRATIVES

Scripture also includes a number of narratives longer than the parables. Here, too, questions of authority and interpretation are not primarily dependent on issues of historical fact. The stories do not claim to present historical fact, but to be stories.

One such narrative is the Book of Job. Our interpretation of that book is aided considerably if we can at least make intelligent guesses about the historical situation *out of which* the book arose. We can guess that the book of Job was written as a response to certain theological claims which had emerged among the Jewish people, claims usually associated with Deuteronomy and the work of the so-called deuteronomistic historians. According to the theology of the deuteronomists, Israel's history could be interpreted as God's equitable dealing with God's people. When defeat or disaster struck, that was God's punishment for apostasy. When Israel flourished, that was God's blessing for fidelity. The Book of Job presents a more complicated picture of the way God deals with humankind. Job is a person who is perfectly upright but who nonetheless suffers grievously.

It may also be that the Book of Job emerged during the period of the exile of the Jewish people in Babylon. Job would then be not only a sign of individual suffering but also a sign of the undeserved suffering of an entire people. The writer, or writers, of Job would be asserting that the suffering of the Jewish people could not rightly be explained as God's judgment and would be seeking some deeper explanation or suggesting that no explanation could possibly suffice.

Our attempts to reconstruct the history out of which Job arose can help us in interpreting the book. However, the book itself does not make any claims to be history. There is no appropriate point in trying to date the birth of Job or the disasters befell him, or of trying to locate Uz on a map of the ancient Near East. The story itself, like the story of the Prodigal son, is told *as* story, and part of its power and authority lies in the richness of its literary devices.

Again we deliberately avoid pretending to say "what Job means," and try instead to suggest some of the devices it uses to tell the story and to involve the readers in what is told.

The beginning and ending of the book are set apart from the book's main dialogue by the fact that they are written in prose. Their style is rather like that of a folk tale. The main points—the information we need to know—are presented without undue detail and without attention to the psychology or motivation of the characters involved.

A section of the prologue takes place in the heavenly council where the Lord gives Satan, who is seen more as his spy than as an evil angel, permission to test Job. Though this places the whole story within the framework of divine intention and purpose, our right reading of the story depends on recognizing that *Job* never knows what went on in the heavenly council, and that even when the Lord appears to Job, the Lord does not reveal the meeting. The discussion between the Lord and Satan is therefore in some ways a literary device: it sets the scene for the dialogue between Job and his friends. It also suggests that the story takes place within God's purpose, but it does not change the fact that for the actors in the story, the nature of God's purpose remains unknowable.

At the end of the story, in good folk tale style, Job is relieved of his suffering, and more than that, all that he has lost is restored twofold. This may seem to vitiate the power of the story, which lies in Job's defiance and puzzlement in the face of undeserved suffering, but as a literary device it seems an appropriate way to end the story. Job has said what Job must say, and there is nothing to be gained by further suffering. He has—in his own odd way—remained faithful and unknowing; faithful and unknowing, he is allowed to live out his last years in comfort.

The poetic dialogue between Job and his three friends carries the great weight of the book. Job's poetry consists in part of puzzlement, in part of protest. His friends' poetry consists in explanation. At the end of the story, the Lord accepts the puzzlement and protest and rejects the explanations:

> After the LORD had spoken these words to Job, the LORD said to Eliphaz the Temanite: "My wrath is kindled against you and against your two friends; for you have not spoken of me what is right, as my servant Job has" (Job 42:7).

Yet within the poetic section of the book it is not clear that Job gets all the best lines or all the best rhetoric. The argument is a real argument, not a mock one. What cuts against the arguments of Job's friends is not the fact that Job argues more powerfully than they, it is the fact that at the end the Lord reveals that Job has spoken rightly, and at the beginning the narrator reveals that Job, contrary to the best guesses of his friends, has done no wrong (Job 1:1). The narrator's introduction and the Lord's conclusion qualify our reading of the dialogue, but the dialogue itself protrays its varied positions with passion and authority.

The final speech is the Lord's, and in response to his speech, Job at last decides to be still (42:1–6; see pp. 75–76). That Job repents is clear enough; why he repents is not so clear. What he has heard from the Lord is a lengthy recitation (perhaps originally two speeches) of the Lord's mighty activity as creator. Is what silences Job simply the almightiness of the Almighty? Is he overpowered? Or is there rather in the images a hint that the Lord is not merely boasting of his might but reminding Job of God's freedom, God's creativity, God's ability to do what God chooses, not out of brute force but out of creative imagination:

> "Where were you when I laid the foundation of the earth?
>   Tell me, if you have understanding.
> Who determined its measurements—surely you know!
>   Or who stretched the line upon it?
> On what were its bases sunk,
>   or who laid its cornerstone,
> when the morning stars sang together,
>   and all the sons of God shouted for joy?"
> "Has the rain a father,
>   or who has begotten the drops of dew?
> From whose womb did the ice come forth,
>   and who has given birth to the hoarfrost of heaven?"
>   (Job 38:4–7, 28–29).

Here God, the father and mother of creation, questions one of creation's children: "Are you my parent, that I should answer to you?"

What does the Book of Job mean? What doctrine does it teach? We cannot simply answer. We can give suggestions, point out possibilities, indicate partial answers. But what the book means it means in large part by being a complex narrative, a narrative including both heaven and earth, both poetry and prose, both divine and human speech. It is a narrative where the divine has its counsels which the human cannot comprehend, and the human has pain which the divine seems never quite to understand. It is a narrative where those who seek to defend the ways of the Lord are condemned as unknowing, and the one who condemns the way of the Lord is defended as speaking truth. Job's material problems are resolved in the simple way of fairy tale: everything lost is now restored twofold. Job's more fundamental problems nag us beyond the quick conclusion of the fairy tale. Why was Job silent, finally? And had he any right to be?

Again the authority comes not through any portrayal of accurate history. The authority comes from the story's ability to involve us, to entice us, to question us, and finally to shift the way in which we see ourselves and the world and the way in which we puzzle about God.

In similar ways we would want to ask how the narrative shapes and enriches the meaning in the Book of Jonah or Daniel, or in the story of Abel and Cain.

Of course the distinction between historical narrative and non-historical narrative cannot simply be maintained. Even when the stuff of history is implied in the stories of Scripture, the shaping of the narrative depends on the imagination and the interpretive power of the narrator. Whatever we may think of the historicity of individual incidents in the Gospel of Mark, it is reasonably clear that it is Mark who has shaped the story to have a particular narrative power, and it is altogether clear that Matthew and Luke have reshaped Mark's story to provide their own rather different version of the Christian narrative.[29]

Whatever we may decide about the historicity of individual events in the stories of the patriarchs or the triumphs of Joseph, the shape of the narrative has been set by the narrator, and to know the meaning of the stories and their authority is partly to know how to read and attend and appreciate the story.

Narrative material at its most powerful derives some of that power from the narrative form. To understand the authority of biblical narrative we need to acknowledge the ways in which stories can inform and shape our lives.

INTERPRETING "FICTIONAL" NARRATIVE TODAY

How can narrative which does not claim to represent historical "facts" have authority for the reflection and practice of contemporary Christians? What I have proposed of the shape and function of the biblical narratives suggests some answers.

BIBLICAL NARRATIVE AND IDENTIFICATION

One characteristic of a powerful story is its ability to bring the reader or listener into its own world. It is not so much that the story need tell of a world precisely like the world the reader knows. It is rather that the story's world is presented with sufficient poignancy and persuasiveness that the reader almost unwittingly enters in. *Hamlet*'s power depends on the audience's ability, if not to feel Hamlet's dilemma as its own, at least to recognize what it would be like to feel Hamlet's dilemma as its own. *Catcher in the Rye* becomes tellingly significant for adolescents generation after generation because they can see Holden Caulfield's world as if it were their world.

So, I have suggested, the power of the story of the Prodigal son rests in the ability of the story to engage the interest and the identification of the hearer. Its special power lies in its ability to engage the reader twice: once in sympathy with the Prodigal, once in sympathy with his brother who stayed at home. The Good Samaritan's story makes the reader identify with the traveler at the side of the road. The parable of the talents causes all but the least modest listener to sympathize with the poor fellow given the smallest trust, ever so prudently stashing the little he had against danger and loss.

Part of the authority which biblical narrative has for us is that it fits us. It is not that we say, "Ah, that's exactly how my life is," but that we say, "My life can give me access to that story; I know how the characters in that world might feel."

When, by faith and imagination, we are given to know how the world of a parable might feel, then the promise or the judgment or the puzzle which the parable provides its characters can become promise, judgment, or puzzle for us. So, for example, the story of Job is not the story of any of its readers. None of us is upright and perfect as that man; few of us have suffered as he did. Yet the power of the narrative, and especially the power of Job's speeches, is such that we can move from our minimal righteousness and our slighter suffering to feel with him the outrage of true righteousness before enormous suffering. Then the question and the promise which come to Job from the whirlwind become comfort and promise for us as well.

BIBLICAL NARRATIVE AND PERCEPTION

There is another angle on the same ability of powerful narrative to involve its audience. It is not only that we are so caught up in the world of the narrative that we feel sympathetic identification with its characters and feel ourselves moved by what happens to them. It is also that the narrative itself, by providing a new world of perceptions and possibilities, shifts our perceptions of the world in which we live.

The playgoer who has been caught up in the performance of *Hamlet* may return to his or her world with a richer sense of the difficulty of moral certainty, the riskiness of choice and the darker riskiness of the refusal to choose, the possibility of sacrifice and the possibility that sacrifice may be gratuitious. Readers of *Catcher in the Rye* perceive their world more wryly for a while—and generations of high school students, for a few days after reading the novel, talk like Holden Caulfield, and therefore *see* somewhat as Holden sees his world.

Rightly to hear the story of the Prodigal son is to move from its world to our world with our perceptions shifted. It is not so much that we know new things as that we see the familiar things more freshly and more tellingly: the modest prodigalities, asking a little freedom at the expense of much responsibility; the little graces, a parent who does not run down the road but does at least grudgingly attempt forgiveness; the vast reluctance to sanction either prodigality or grace—these features of the world were there before the parable, but we did not attend to them. After the parable they intrude upon us, and attention must be paid.

It is not only the events of the story or its personages which shift perceptions. At levels more subtle and perhaps more pervasive the story's very language shifts both our language and our understanding. The playgoer who hears Hamlet cry, "The rest is silence" (Shakespeare, *Hamlet*, Act V, sc. 2, line 372), may forget the line or just who said it, but from there on attends to death and silence somewhat differently. The Prodigal's language has become the common language of our thought: "far country," "older brother," "fatted calf." The nuances have become the nuances by which we see things as they are. Things are as they are because we see them with that story in our minds, or just beneath our minds.

The reader has heard Job's argument with God and finally hears God's argument with Job:

"Who shut in the sea with doors,
    when it burst forth from the womb;
when I made clouds its garment,
    and thick darkness its swaddling band,

and prescribed bounds for it,
   and set bars and doors,
and said, 'Thus far shall you come, and no farther,
   and here shall your proud waves be stayed'? . . .
"Have you commanded the morning since your days began,
   and caused the dawn to know its place,
that it might take hold of the skirts of the earth,
   and the wicked be shaken out of it?" (Job 38:8–13).

If the story has been carefully attended to and God's speech is imaginatively heard, the hearer's perceptions change. It is not that he or she emerges from the narrative with a new doctrine of God or a better hypothesis on the origins of the universe. It is rather that the familiar realities are perceived in a new light. One still prays to God, but more modestly. One still enjoys the sea or notices the rising sun, but both appear in a new light. They are different in the nuances they evoke; they are different in the ways they hint of the power and the creativity of God.

Probably few are the readers who can write essays on God and creation as revealed in Job 38, but to hear Job 38 as the climax to a great and complex narrative is to believe God and see creation differently. The authority of narrative is the authority which shifts our sight.

BIBLICAL NARRATIVE AND QUESTION

Because narrative has particular power to involve and to refocus our perceptions, narrative has particular power to call us (and our perceptions) into question. That, of course, is precisely what God's speech does for Job in Job 38.

Then the LORD answered Job out of the whirlwind:
"Who is this that darkens counsel by words without knowledge?
Gird up your loins like a man,
   I will question you, and you shall declare to me.
Where were you when I laid the foundation of the earth?
   Tell me, if you have understanding . . ." (Job 38:1–4).

The questioning of Job is particularly poignant because Job has indeed questioned God in those impassioned chapters which preceded this one. The reader, caught up in Job's questioning, is taken aback by being suddenly questioned.

We have noted that the end of the parable of the Prodigal son leaves the elder brother questioned: "Will you join the party? Will you join in the joy at your brother's return and your father's mercy?" The question is unanswered within the framework of the parable itself, and so it becomes a question for the listener. By the parable the listener is finally questioned. The lack of resolution becomes a challenge: Will it be justice or mercy? How do I choose?

As Luke tells the story of the Good Samaritan, Jesus explicitly questions the audience, "Which of these three, do you think, proved neighbor to the man who fell among the robbers?" (Luke 10:36). The story itself has set other questions, too. How do we react when we imagine ourselves denied help by those we should most expect to give it and offered help by one we most assume will deny it? What happens to our self-understanding when we begin feeling the pain of the man caught at the side of the road and are asked to feel the compassion of one whom we are determined not to find sympathetic at all?

Sometimes the power of narrative lies precisely in its unwillingness to resolve fundamental puzzles. Sometimes the power of narrative lies in its ability to dissuade us from false resolutions and rightly to puzzle us again. The old cliche that "Christ is the answer" runs hard against the Christ who speaks in parables. Sometimes Christ is the question, and the questioner as well.

BIBLICAL NARRATIVE AND CONVERSION

In his book on Christian narrative, Stroup argues that the power of Christian stories sometimes lies precisely in the way in which they do not fit our ordinary experience but transform that experience:

> We have insisted that the encounter between personal identity and Christian narrative is best described in terms of the metaphor of "collision" precisely because the encounter is not necessarily adequate to human experience but jarring and world transforming. . . . Hence the very "appropriateness" of Christian faith may be that it is inappropriate to human experience and demands a fundamental reinterpretation of personal history and personal identity.[30]

In the book of Job, to the extent that we identify with Job's experience and Job's complaints, we are at least challenged by what can only be described as Job's conversion:

> Then Job answered the LORD:
> "I know that thou canst do all things,
>   and that no purpose of thine can be thwarted.
> 'Who is this that hides counsel without knowledge?'
> Therefore I have uttered what I did not understand,
>   things too wonderful for me, which I did not know.
> 'Hear, and I will speak;
>   I will question you, and you declare to me.'

I had heard of thee by the hearing of the ear,
  but now my eye sees thee;
therefore I despise myself,
  and repent in dust and ashes" (Job 42:1–6).

(This has served precisely as a challenge for many interpreters of Job, who find his anguish more convincing than his repentance. There are good theological reasons for the problem and familiar aesthetic ones. Anguish is easier to portray vividly than is repentance.)

The way in which Luke ends the story of the Good Samaritan makes that stress on conversion and transformation explicit (Luke 10:25–37). A young man comes to Jesus and asks the essential questions of salvation: "What shall I do to inherit eternal life?" Jesus immediately puts the burden of the answer on the man himself: "How do you read (the law)?" The man answers, "You shall love the Lord your God with all your heart, and with all your soul, and with all your strength, and with all your mind, and your neighbor as yourself." And Jesus said to him: "You have answered right; do this, and you shall live."

Again the lawyer seeks to avoid the responsibility for transformation. "He, desiring to justify himself, said to Jesus: 'And who is my neighbor?'" The story is told precisely to pull the ground out from under the lawyer. He is no longer allowed to distance himself from the question of his own salvation. What he decides, how he acts, is essential to the life he seeks. The story ends, as we have seen, with Jesus' question to the lawyer: "Which of these three, do you think, proved neighbor to the man who fell among the robbers?" The lawyer said, "The one who showed mercy on him." Then comes the call for conversion, for transformation: "Go and do likewise."

It is almost certainly Matthew who ends the parable of the workers who come late to the vineyard with an originally separate saying of Jesus: "So the last will be first, and the first last (Matt. 20:16). Yet the Matthean editing catches something of the radical nature of the parable. It proclaims a kingdom which reverses expectations. If the parable has worked upon its audience, their expectations have been shifted. What seemed to them of first importance is now of no import at all; what seemed to them trivial has become central and all-encompassing. The importance of earning one's just way is nothing compared to the centrality of the ungrudging generosity of God.

Norman Perrin described tellingly the way in which parables, and we might add other biblical narratives, may collide with the world of their audience:

They challenge the hearer to explore the manifold possibilities of the experience of God as king, and they do so in ways which constantly remind the hearer that, on the one hand, God is to be experienced in the historicality of the world of everyday, while, on the other hand, they claim that God is to be experienced precisely in the shattering of that everyday world. Moreover, they do this in ways which constantly leave the hearer naked and alone before the possibility and challenge of the experience of God as king.[31]

The authority of the biblical narratives lies partly in their power to shift the world and the consciousness of the hearer. It is not that we test their authenticity by our own experience, it is that we discover what authentic experience is by hearing and attending them.

BIBLICAL NARRATIVE AND PRESENCE

Perhaps the most elusive aspect of the authority of biblical narrative is the way in which such narratives can suggest or mediate the presence of that fundamental reality to which they refer. The quotation from Perrin indicates that sometimes the converting power of the parable lies in its ability to make *present* the boundary experience to which it refers. The parables "leave the hearer naked and alone before the possibility and challenge of the experience of God as king."[32]

When Job says to the Lord, who has addressed him from the whirlwind, "I had heard of thee by the hearing of the ear, but now my eye sees thee" (Job 42:5), Job may speak for the reader as well. We may not have *seen* the Lord in the whirlwind, but if the narrative has worked aright we have heard the Lord; and the rich imagery of the Lord's argument against Job may even enable us to see the divine majesty as well.

The parables which the gospels relate are always related as Jesus' parables. That reality to which the stories point is embodied in the storyteller. Rightly to understand them is to understand them as being inextricably related to him; and rightly to hear them may be to hear him as made present *in* them. So, for instance, the three "parables" of Matthew 25 are actually only two parables. The parables of the bridegroom and of the landlord who pass judgment on belief and unbelief find their significance in the revelation of the third parable, that the one who judges faith and unfaithfulness, the one hinted in the bridegroom and the landlord, is the Son of Man. And the reader knows it is the Son of Man who speaks the parable as well.

In John's gospel the identification becomes explicit time after time. Parables become self-descriptions of the Lord, ways of declaring his presence. The parable of bread is a parable about the sustaining power of Jesus' word (John 6). The parable of the vine is a parable about his relationship to the church (John 15). John's version of the parable of the shepherd (John 10) makes explicit what is only implicit in Matthew and Luke. The one good shepherd who protects his own is the one who tells the parable, Jesus himself. Finally, that protecting of his own involves the loss of the shepherd's life for the sake of the flock.

All the gospels hint what John's gospel says. Rightly to hear the parables is to acknowledge the one who tells the parables. The authority of parables is partly the authority of the one who speaks them. His being present in his parables gives them their peculiar authority.

Biblical narratives therefore derive their authority from their ability to entice the hearer to identify with their characters. They may derive their authority from the way in which the world they present causes the reader to perceive his or her own world differently and anew. They may derive their authority from the ways in which they ask questions of the hearer and finally put the hearer's life in question. They may derive their authority from their power to collide with the hearer's world and consciousness and finally to convert the hearer to a new world and a richer self-understanding. They derive their most powerful authority when they mediate something of that reality of which they speak, when stories of the kingdom shock us into acknowledgement of the kingdom's presence, and the parables of Jesus are not only the reminders of what he said but also the presentation of who he is.

Though I have distinguished between historical narrative and fictional narrative for the purposes of this chapter, it need hardly be added that narratives more closely rooted to history than the parables of Job may perform something of the same functions they have performed. The story of King David can and does provide places for identification, shifted perception, questioning, and perhaps even conversion and presence. The gospels derive their power not only from the history to which they witness but from the powerful ways in which the evangelists present that history. The gospels are authoritative not only because they point to the nature of a specific life lived among us, but because they provide those ways in which that life can touch, shift, question, and convert the lives of those who read the gospels. Like the parables, the gospels rightly read (and heard and preached) find their final authority when the one whom they present is acknowledged to be present with those who read and hear.

NOTES

1. For the former sort of analysis, cf. G. Ernest Wright and Reginald Fuller, *The Book of the Acts of God* (Garden City, N.Y.: Doubleday & Co., Anchor Books, 1957, 1960), 3–15; for the stress on narrative as the essential clue to biblical literature, cf. Hans Frei, *The Eclipse of Biblical Narrative* (New Haven: Yale University Press, 1974) and G. W. Stroup, *The Promise of Narrative Theology* (Atlanta: John Knox Press, 1981); narrative is also the second form of discourse discussed in the essay by Ricoeur, "Toward a Hermeneutic of the Idea of Revelation," in *Essays on Biblical Interpretation*, ed. Lewis S. Mudge (Philadelphia: Fortress Press, 1980), 77–81.

2. William S. McFeely, *Grant: A Biography* (New York: Norton, 1981), 6.

3. McFeely, *Grant*, 3, xii. I am aware, of course, that no historian writes without pre-judgments, special interests, or peculiar concerns. Indeed McFeely is particularly candid about his interest in exploring Grant's (appalling) attitude to race relations and testing the hypothesis that one reason for the Civil War was that many ordinary and energetic Americans like Grant saw themselves as failures and needed something to do with their energy and drive for success. From both of these interpretations he draws fairly clear cautionary lessons for his compatriots. "[Grant's story] suggests that we must rethink both the worth of war and the uses we make of politics if we are to build a society in which a Ulysses Grant can be heard in a constructive way" (522). So the history is not "pure" history, nor does such a thing exist. However, McFeely's fundamental purpose is to present as clearly as possible the man himself, and that I think would be the fundamental purpose neither of the Books of Samuel nor of Luke's Gospel.

4. Gerhard von Rad, *Old Testament Theology*, Vol. I, Eng. trans. D. M. G. Stalker (New York: Harper & Row, 1962), 316.

5. Brevard Childs, *Introduction to the Old Testament as Scripture* (Philadelphia: Fortress Press, 1979), 29.

6. For perhaps the most influential study of Luke's theological concerns, cf. Hans Conzelmann, *The Theology of St. Luke,* Eng. trans. Geoffrey Buswell (Philadelphia: Fortress Press, 1982).

7. There is a bias inherent in this interpretation which I tend to share, but can recognize as a bias nonetheless. If a biblical prophecy corresponds with remarkable accuracy to the subsequent history to which it refers, the tendency of critics is to assume that the prophecy has been shaped or reshaped in the light of that history. One reason scholars think Luke's Gospel was written after the fall of Jerusalem is that Jesus' prediction of that fall corresponds so closely to the events themselves that it must have been rewritten in the light of the events. The alternative explanation is of course possible—that some prophetic material in the Old and New Testaments did in fact predict with remarkable accuracy the events which were to succeed that prophecy. One's skepticism about this is informed, I think, not only by the canons of conventional historical wisdom (prophecy doesn't work that way) but by a theological understanding of prophecy, which—for somewhat different reasons—also thinks that prophecy doesn't generally work that way. Cf. chapter two above.

8. This problem is not peculiar to Scripture; it is true of much ancient

literature. We do not have many separate sources to use to test Plutarch's *Lives*, for example, or Plato's portrait of Socrates.

9. I discuss various options at somewhat greater length as they relate to the question of Jesus' resurrection in my book *Fact and Faith* (Valley Forge, Pa.: Judson Press, 1975), 85-91.

10. Carl F. H. Henry, *In God, Revelation, and Authority*, Vol. II (Waco, Tex.: Word Books, 1976), 311.

11. Henry, *God, Revelation, and Authority*, II:312-22.

12. Frei, *Eclipse of Biblical Narrative;* cf., e.g., 281.

13. Frei, *Eclipse of Biblical Narrative*, viii.

14. Karl Barth, *Church Dogmatics*, I:ii, Eng. trans. G. T. Thompson and Harold Knight (Edinburgh: T. and T. Clark, 1936, 1956), 373.

15. Rudolf Bultmann, *History and Eschatology* (New York: Harper & Row, Harper Torchbook, 1957, 1962), 151-52.

16. Schubert Ogden, *Christ Without Myth* (New York: Harper and Bros., 1961), 181.

17. Stroup, *Narrative Theology*, 234.

18. Nils Dahl, *The Crucified Messiah and Other Essays* (Minneapolis: Augsburg Publishing House, 1974), 77.

19. Cf. Ricoeur, "Toward a Hermeneutic," 78.

20. T. S. Eliot, "Burnt Norton," in *Four Quartets* from *The Complete Poems and Plays 1909-1950* (New York: Harcourt Brace & World, Inc., 1952), 118.

21. This does not mean that the historical circumstances which gave rise to the story and the historical and cultural details which help interpret the story may not be helpful to our understanding. It does help to interpret the Book of Job if we decide that it is written partly in response to the theology expressed in the deuteronomic writings and represents a meditation on the suffering of the exile. It does help us to understand the story of the Good Samaritan if we remember the historical circumstance of the antipathy between Jews and Samaritans and the setting of the story within the ministry of Jesus, who was notorious for ignoring traditional social barriers.

22. Cf. Joachim Jeremias, *The Parables of Jesus*, Eng. trans. S. H. Hooke (New York: Charles Scribner's Sons; London: SCM Press, 1963), 77-79; John Dominic Crossan, *In Parables: The Challenge of the Historical Jesus* (New York: Harper & Row, 1973), 39-44; and C. H. Dodd, *The Parables of the Kingdom* (New York: Charles Scribner's Sons; London: Collins, 1935, 1961), 3.

23. Allegorical interpretation, however, was not altogether triumphant in the "pre-critical" history of biblical exegesis. John Calvin writes of Augustine's allegory on the Good Samaritan and of several other allegorical interpretations of that parable: "We should have more reverence for Scripture than to allow ourselves to transfigure its sense so freely. Anyone may see that these speculations have been cooked up by meddlers, quite divorced from the mind of Christ." *New Testament Commentaries, On the Gospels*, III, Eng. trans. A. W. Morrison (Grand Rapids: Wm. B. Eerdmans, 1972), 39.

24. The first edition of Jülicher's book, *Die Gleichnessreden Jesu*, was published in 1886. The most recent edition is a photographic copy of the 1910 edition (Darmstadt: Wissenschaftliche Buchgesellschaft, 1963).

25. On this and on the relationship between this broad moral point and the parable as interpretation of the kingdom, cf. Norman Perrin, *Jesus and the Language of the Kingdom* (Philadelphia: Fortress Press, 1976), 93–96; Werner Georg Kümmel, *The New Testament: The History of the Investigation of its Problems,* Eng. trans. S. M. L. Gilmour and H. C. Kee (Nashville: Abingdon Press, 1972), 188; Jeremias, *Parables of Jesus,* 19; Dodd, *Parables of the Kingdom,* 12.

26. Cf. Dodd, *Parables of the Kingdom,* 18–20, 34–35; Jeremias, *Parables of Jesus,* 23, 30, 38, 42.

27. Cf. Perrin, *Jesus and the Language,* esp. chap. 3; Amos N. Wilder, *Early Christian Rhetoric* (Cambridge, Mass.: Harvard University Press, 1971), esp. chap. 5; Crossan, *In Parables;* Sallie McFague, *Speaking in Parables* (Philadelphia: Fortress Press, 1975).

28. W. H. Auden, "In Memory of W. B. Yeats (d. Jan. 1939)," in *Collected Shorter Poems* (New York: Random House, Vintage, 1975), 143.

29. On Mark as a narrative, cf. especially Frank Kermode, *The Genesis of Secrecy: On the Interpretation of Narrative* (Cambridge, Mass.: Harvard University Press, 1979); Robert M. Fowler, *Loaves and Fishes* (Chico, Calif.: Scholars Press, 1981), 149–79.

30. Stroup, *Narrative Theology,* 235–36.

31. Perrin, *Jesus and the Language,* 199.

32. Perrin, *Jesus and the Language,* 199.

4 / The Authority of Wisdom

While prophetic literature presents God's words to humankind and narrative literature portrays God's activity within human history, wisdom literature deals more centrally with human insights and understanding.[1] The literature which is commonly called wisdom literature includes Proverbs, Ecclesiastes, and Job. We shall see that certain sayings of Jesus and some portions of Paul's letters also show characteristics of wisdom sayings.[2]

WISDOM LITERATURE IN THE OLD TESTAMENT

It is very difficult to place precisely either the provenance or the date of specific sayings or collections of wisdom literature.[3]

One clue to Israel's understanding of wisdom lies in the fact that in their present form both Proverbs and parts of Ecclesiastes are attributed to or associated with Solomon and his court.

Proverbs begins with this editorial inscription: "The Proverbs of Solomon, son of David, king of Israel" (Prov. 1:1). Ecclesiastes begins with a similar attribution: "The Words of the Preacher, the son of David, king in Jerusalem" (Eccl. 1:1). Then the writer of Ecclesiastes places some of his sayings in a context which is supposed to recall the reader to the court of the great King.

> I said to myself, "I have acquired great wisdom, surpassing all who were over Jerusalem before me; and my mind has had great experience of wisdom and knowledge."
>
> I made great works; I built houses and planted vineyards for myself; I made myself gardens and parks, and planted in them all kinds of fruit trees. I made myself pools from which to water the forest of growing trees. I bought male and female slaves, and had slaves who were born in my house; I had also great possessions of herds and flocks, more than any who had been before me in Jerusalem. I also gathered for myself silver and gold and the treasure of kings and provinces; I got singers, both men and women, and many concubines, man's delight.
>
> So I became great and surpassed all who were before me in Jerusalem; also my wisdom remained with me (Eccl. 1:16; 2:4–9).

In both Proverbs and Ecclesiastes it is clear that Solomon has become a paradigm of the wise man. Those who wish to affirm "traditional" wisdom (as in Proverbs) and those who wish to undercut such wisdom (as in Ecclesiastes) see Solomon as a model for generations of wise men to come.

The portrait of Solomon as the paradigmatic wise man may well be derived from the narrative in 1 Kings 3, where the Lord appears to Solomon at Gibeon:

> At Gibeon the LORD appeared to Solomon in a dream by night; and God said, "Ask what I shall give you." And Solomon said, " . . . thou hast made thy servant king in place of David my father, although I am but a little child; I do not know how to go out or come in. . . . Give thy servant therefore an understanding mind to govern thy people, that I may discern between good and evil; for who is able to govern this thy great people?
>
> It pleased the LORD that Solomon had asked this. And God said to him, "Because you have asked this, and have not asked for yourself long life or riches or the life of your enemies, but have asked for yourself understanding to discern what is right, behold I now do according to your word. Behold, I give you a wise and discerning mind, so that none like you has been before you and none like you shall arise after you" (1 Kings 3:5–12).[4]

It seems fairly clear that many of the sayings we have within wisdom literature, especially in the book of Proverbs, derive from a variety of settings, including both the royal court and popular proverbial literature. Furthermore, some of the wisdom sayings almost certainly derive from international contexts and were borrowed by Israel's writers and compilers. However, the use of Solomon as a paradigm indicates that those who edited Proverbs and Ecclesiastes identified with a particular stream of tradition and with particular figures within the community of Israel who considered themselves to be "wise men." Just as Israel depended on the word of the prophets, so, too, Israel learned from the observations and insights of these wise men, who may in fact have associated with one another in "schools," and who certainly compiled wisdom sayings and passed them on from generation to generation.

We can understand something of the nature and scope of wisdom in Israel's community by attending to the literature contained with the book of Proverbs. Several features of wisdom literature are pertinent to our discussion.

First, at least on one level, wisdom literature is less concerned with what God reveals to humankind (either through words to the prophets or through mighty acts in history) than with what humankind can discover about the world through the use of human wisdom. Some of the most striking proverbs make no claim to represent "words from the Lord" but rather indicate what discerning people can notice from careful observation of the world around them.

The careful observation may be observation of the ways of human relationships: "A soft answer turns away wrath, but a harsh word stirs up anger" (Prov. 15:1). The observation may be an observation of the realities of economics: "A slack hand causes poverty, but the hand of the diligent makes rich" (Prov. 10:4). The careful observation may be a caustic recognition of the varieties of human folly: "Like vinegar to the teeth, and smoke to the eyes, so is the sluggard to those who send him" (Prov. 10:26); and, "Like a gold ring in a swine's snout is a beautiful woman without discretion" (Prov. 11:22).

In Ecclesiastes the specific observations about varieties of human folly are used to illustrate the larger claim which frames the book: "Vanity of vanities, says the Preacher, vanity of vanities! All is vanity" (Eccl. 1:2). Folly becomes, not one possibility within the range of human behavior, but rather the pervasive mark of the human endeavor, since not even the shrewdest attempts to be wise can escape the pitfalls of folly. "For in much wisdom is much vexation, and he who increases knowledge increases sorrow" (Eccl. 1:18).[5]

So fundamental is the role of human observation in the wisdom literature that some have seen that literature as fundamentally "secular," concerned not with the dealings of God but with the workings of the world.[6] We shall suggest below that wisdom literature does have basic theological presuppositions, but the literature is "secular" in the sense that its fundamental strategy is to show the reader what the wise man has discovered about the world around him. It begins with human recognition rather than divine revelation. R. B. Y. Scott affirms that, "Broadly speaking, the prophet speaks from the standpoint of revelation, the wise man from that of reason working from the data of experience and observation."[7]

A second feature of wisdom literature is that it presupposes that there are various *orders* to experience and that the perceptive observer can discern something of those regularities.

The classical instance of such a claim is found in Eccl. 3:1–8.

For everything there is a season,
and a time for every matter under heaven:
a time to be born, and a time to die;
a time to plant, and a time to pluck up what is planted;
a time to kill, and a time to heal;

a time to break down, and a time to build up;
a time to weep, and a time to laugh;
a time to mourn, and a time to dance;
a time to cast away stones, and a time to gather
  stones together;
a time to embrace, and a time to refrain from embracing;
a time to seek, and a time to lose;
a time to keep, and a time to cast away;
a time to rend, and a time to sew;
a time to keep silence, and a time to speak;
a time to love, and a time to hate;
a time for war, and a time for peace.

Then, characteristically, the writer draws a discouraging moral from the regularity he describes: "What gain has the worker from his toil?" (Eccl. 3:9; similarly see Eccl. 1:4–9).

In the book of Proverbs, Gerhard von Rad points out, "The counting and listing of things, of types of behaviour, of virtues, etc., is an elementary need of man in his search for order. . . . In the case of the so-called numerical saying it is with this desire for order, planted deep within man, that we have to do, particularly in a quite specific form of proverb which was cultivated not only in Israel but also in other lands of the ancient Near East."[8]

Sometimes the perceived order is in social structures:

Under three things the earth trembles;
  under four it cannot bear up:
a slave when he becomes king,
  and a fool when he is filled with food;
an unloved woman when she gets a husband,
  and a maid when she succeeds her mistress (Prov. 30:21–23).

Sometimes the perceived order is in natural order:

Four things on earth are small,
  but they are exceedingly wise:
the ants are a people not strong,
  yet they provide their food in the summer;
the badgers are a people not mighty,
  yet they make their homes in the rocks;
the locusts have no king,
  yet all of them march in rank;
the lizard you can take in your hands,
  yet it is in kings' palaces (Prov. 30:24–28).

In this latter instance the natural description also includes a social note: even king's palaces have lizards to contend with. Other lists of proverbial wisdom combine natural and social observation, and imply that the order of the natural world finds its analogue in the world of politics (e.g., Prov. 30:29–31).

The third feature of wisdom consists of stress upon what we can call "common sense." Wisdom represents common sense because it represents *ordinary* sense. The wise men are not wise because they fit the contemporary model of the innovative scientist who devises new hypotheses and tests the hypotheses by bold experiment. The wise men are wise because they are receptive to the experience which is all around them. They see what is there to be seen and what they can call on other reasonably wise people to see. The wise are distinguished from the foolish precisely because the foolish have no common sense. They cannot see the world for what it obviously is.[9]

Prov. 26:20 represents a careful observation both of the natural world and of human relationships and draws the comparison, "For lack of wood the fire goes out; and where there is no whisperer, quarreling ceases." Again Prov. 25:19 is a warning based in common, ordinary sense: "Trust in a faithless man in time of trouble is like a bad tooth or a foot that slips."

Fools are marked as fools precisely because they lack common sense. They can be compared to animals at their silliest: "Like a dog that returns to his vomit is a fool that repeats his folly" (Prov. 26:11).

Wisdom also represents common sense because it represents *shared* sense. Especially in the composition of the book of Proverbs (but also in some of the editorial notes in Ecclesiastes) there is evidence that the wisdom gathered here represents a *tradition* of seeing and commenting on the world. Observations are presented as representations of a heritage of wisdom; and they are presented on the assumption that the wise reader will nod in assent. Common sense is wisdom which people hold in common. That sense of tradition, of commonality, is perhaps most evident in the address of some of the proverbs:

> My son, keep your father's commandment,
>   and forsake not your mother's teaching.
> For the commandment is a lamp and the teaching a light,
>   and the reproofs of discipline are the way of life (Prov. 6:20, 23).

Von Rad points to the shared aspects of wisdom, and both to the strengths and the possible weaknesses of this kind of "common" sense:

> (Experiential) knowledge does not accrue to an individual, nor even to a generation. It acquires its status and its binding claim only when it appears as the common possession of a nation or of a broad stratum within a nation. But

precisely in its quality as a communal possession this knowledge finds itself on dangerous ground. Certainly, on the basis of a long period of trial, it can make for itself a claim to stability and validity. But, insofar as it becomes the possession of all, it is in danger of simplifying and generalizing truths that can be generalized only to a certain extent. . . . Dangers threaten everywhere, threaten not only the process of self-disclosure but also the intellectual arranging and developing of what has been experienced.[10]

(In this sense we might see Job's friends as the speakers for accumulated and shared wisdom, and Job as the novel counterexample to that very good conventional wisdom. Job argues that "very good" conventional wisdom is not good enough. The writer of Ecclesiastes takes all the conventional observations—the regularity of the world and the similarity of its orders—and draws the novel conclusion: Nothing avails.)

In the fourth case, we note that the wisdom writers are not unaware that "common sense" has its limitations, and indeed one pervasive motif in Proverbs, Ecclesiastes, and Job is that human wisdom is always limited, always comes up against the inscrutable. The inscrutable, most often, is held to belong to the provenance of God.

The sense of limitation upon wisdom is represented in a number of different aspects. Sometimes the stress is on the limit to any human enterprise before the mysteries of the wisdom and planning of God: "The horse is made ready for the day of battle, but the victory belongs to the Lord" (Prov. 21:31). Sometimes the limits of wisdom may divide what is intended from what is accomplished within a human endeavor: "The plans of the mind belong to man, but the answer of the tongue is from the Lord" (Prov. 16:1).

Both the confidence of the writers of Proverbs and the skepticism of the writer of Ecclesiastes acknowledge that a basic limitation is placed upon human understanding by the deeper purposes of God.

It is the glory of God to conceal things,
  but the glory of kings is to search things out (Prov. 25:2).

When I applied my mind to known wisdom, and to see the business that is done on earth, how neither day nor night one's eyes see sleep; then I saw all the work of God, that man cannot find out the work that is done under the sun. However much man may toil in seeking, he will not find it out; even though a wise man claims to know, he cannot find it out (Eccl. 8:16–17).

The great poem on Wisdom herself in Job 28 asserts by its imagery what wisdom literature generally maintains, that human wisdom is always *limited* by the wisdom of God.

"But where shall wisdom be found?
    And where is the place of understanding?
Man does not know the way to it,
    and it is not found in the land of the living.
"God understands the way to it,
    and he knows the place,
For he looks to the ends of the earth,
    and sees everything under the heavens" (Job 28:12–13, 23–24).

The fifth feature of wisdom literature which we need to consider is the characteristic style of the literature. While it is clear that the proverbs and stories and poems of the wisdom writers have implications for the way in which the readers are to live their lives, nevertheless, as von Rad indicates,

> . . . their style is not directly didactic. Far and away the majority of them are statements which make assertions in thetical form quite neutrally, that is without any direct appeal to the listeners. They are not imperative in character but have, rather, a retrospective tendency and have, basically, only empirical value. In their own way and within their own sphere they simply wish to establish something positive, something unquestionably valid. The experiences are cited, the conclusions are drawn, and the result is produced.[11]

So, for instance, we can see the moral applications of the following wisdom sayings, but the applications are implied, they are not stated as commands.

A friend loves at all times,
    and a brother is born for adversity (Prov. 17:17).
Even a fool who keeps silent is considered wise;
    when he closes his lips, he is deemed intelligent (Prov. 17:28).
    The words of the wise heard in quiet are better than the shouting of a ruler among fools. Wisdom is better than weapons of war, but one sinner destroys much good (Eccl. 9:17–18).

Quite often the wisdom sayings are expressed in poetic parallelism. The second line of the saying either repeats the first with slightly different nuances, or contrasts with the first, or supplements the first by adding some quite new dimension of insight. The style relies on careful observation of the way the world goes, and therefore the comparative devices themselves illustrate the ability of wisdom to discern the nature of human activity.

A false witness will not go unpunished,
    and he who utters lies will not escape (Prov. 19:5; cited in von Rad, p. 27).
When it goes well with the righteous, the city rejoices;
    and when the wicked perish there are shouts of gladness (Prov. 11:10).

Some wisdom sayings simply represent comparisons: the simple presentation of two elements, each of which throws light on the other.

Clouds, wind, but yet no rain,
a man who boasts of a gift he does not have (Prov. 25:14; cited in von Rad,
p. 29).

Sometimes the comparison is a bit more complex:

A little sleep, a little slumber,
a little folding of the hands to rest,
and poverty will come upon you like a vagabond,
and want like an armed man (Prov. 6:10-11).

Even those wisdom sayings which are in the imperative mood usually give some reason, some motivation for the imperative, and this motivation indicates the extent to which the insights of wisdom are based on an understanding of the way the world goes:

Be not one of those who give pledges,
who become surety for debts.
If you have nothing with which to pay,
why should your bed be taken from under you? (Prov. 22:26-27).

The style of wisdom literature, therefore, is appropriate to one of its major presuppositions. Wisdom literature is based in large measure on observation: how do things go in the world? What effects will certain actions have? The devices of parallelism and comparison allow the wisdom writer to demonstrate how carefully and astutely he has observed the world around him. He can draw parallels and make connections between phenomena, and these parallels and connections help the reader to understand better the world and to respond more prudently and wisely.

In the sixth case we note that at one level much of the wisdom literature emphasizes the gifts of human wisdom, knowledge, discernment, prudence. The strong sense we have seen in prophetic literature of God's speaking quite directly to the human situation is largely missing. The strong stress we saw in the narrative literature on God's direct activity within human affairs is largely missing. Yet this is not to say that there are not fundamental theological elements lying behind the wisdom literature.[12]

In sum, the central theological claim behind the wisdom literature is that God is the creator of the world, its phenomena and its orders, and that therefore even as wisdom deals with the world it deals with the God who created that world:

> Consider the work of God;
> who can make straight what he has made crooked?
> In the day of prosperity be joyful, and in the day of adversity consider; God has made the one as well as the other, so that man may not find out anything that will be after him (Eccl. 7:13–14).
> The LORD has made everything for its purpose,
> even the wicked for the day of trouble (Prov. 16:4).

It is because God is creator of the phenomena and the orders of the world that there is always a limit to human wisdom. The best attempts of human discernment and the best behavior based on human prudence are still faced with the unsearchable decrees or decisions of God.

> "But where shall wisdom be found?
> And where is the place of understanding?
> Man does not know the way to it,
> and it is not found in the land of the living" (Job 28:12–13).
> A man's mind plans his way,
> but the LORD directs his steps (Prov. 16:9).
> When I applied my mind to know wisdom, and to see the business that is done on earth, how neither day nor night one's eyes see sleep; then I saw all the work of God, that man cannot find out the work that is done under the sun. However much man may toil in seeking, he will not find it out; even though a wise man claims to know, he cannot find it out (Eccl. 8:16–17).

In some of the wisdom sayings, God is not only the creator of the world and its orders, God also plays an active role in ongoing human activity, particularly in punishing evil and rewarding righteousness or wisdom. The question is not really raised whether this activity on God's part is to be seen as intervention in the workings of the world or as a working out of God's purposes precisely in the regularities of human life. Yet God is not here simply relegated to the role of an observer of human affairs.

> Do not rob the poor, because he is poor,
> or crush the afflicted at the gate;
> for the LORD will plead their cause
> and despoil of life those who despoil them (Prov. 22:22).
> The LORD tears down the house of the proud,
> but maintains the widow's boundaries (Prov. 15:25).

Ecclesiastes thinks also that the hand of God may deal with human activity but can find no moral reason behind God's dealings.

> But all this I laid to heart, examining it all, how the righteous and the wise and their deeds are in the hand of God; whether it is love or hate man does not know. Everything before them is vanity, since one fate comes to all, to the righteous and the wicked, to the good and the evil. . . . As is the good man, so is the sinner; and he who swears is as he who shuns an oath. This is an evil in all that is done under the sun, that one fate comes to all . . . (Eccl. 9:1–3a).

Because wisdom literature deals finally with the God who creates the world and its orders and because wisdom literature deals finally with the God who provides weal and woe for humankind, the deepest wisdom is also a kind of piety. It is a piety which acknowledges the limits of human wisdom before the boundless and inscrutable purposes of God.

So the editor of Proverbs includes the following climax in the introduction:

> The fear of the LORD is the beginning of knowledge;
> fools despise wisdom and instruction (Prov. 1:7).

The editor of Ecclesiastes, seeking to soften the harshness of the original author of the book, adds a cautionary conclusion:

> The end of the matter; all has been heard. Fear God, and keep his commandments; for this is the whole duty of man. For God will bring every deed into judgment, with every secret thing, whether good or evil (Eccl. 12:13–14).

The great poem on Wisdom in Job 28, which describes the human inability to find wisdom and ascribes true wisdom to the knowledge and decree of God, ends with this word from the Lord to the seeker of wisdom:

> "'Behold, the fear of the LORD, that is wisdom;
> and to depart from evil is understanding'" (Job 28:28).

Because wisdom literature includes both the strong stress on human observation and prudence and the reminder that human wisdom is limited by the fear of God and that the deepest wisdom is also a kind of trust, von Rad finds in the wisdom literature a kind of paradoxical description of appropriate human life:

> Reduced to its bare essentials, these regulations (of the wise men) for a fruitful life seem determined by a remarkable dialectic. Do not hesitate to summon up all your powers in order to familiarize yourself with all the rules which might somehow be effective in life. Ignorance in any form will be detrimental to you; only the "fool" thinks he can shut his eyes to this. Experience, on the other hand, teaches that you can never be certain. You must always remain open for a completely new experience. You will never

become really wise, for in the last resort, this life of yours is determined not by rules, but by God.[13]

Finally, the most elaborate claim regarding the relationship of wisdom to God the creator suggests that wisdom was present with God at the beginning of creation as a reality distinct from the specific orders and phenomena of creation.[14]

Prov. 1:20 represents wisdom by the literary device of personification: "Wisdom cries aloud in the street; in the markets she raises her voice." In Proverbs 8 the writer moves beyond literary device to make a substantive claim about the relationship of Wisdom to God:

"The LORD created me at the beginning of his work,
    the first of his acts of old.
Ages ago I was set up,
    at the first, before the beginning of the earth.
When there were no depths I was brought forth,
    when there were no springs abounding with water. . . .
when he marked out the foundations of the earth,
    then I was beside him, like a master workman;
and I was daily his delight,
    rejoicing before him always,
rejoicing in his inhabited world
    and delighting in the sons of men.
And now, my sons, listen to me:
    happy are those who keep my ways. . . .
For he who finds me finds life
    and obtains favor from the LORD;
but he who misses me injures himself;
    all who hate me love death" (Prov. 8:22–36).

It must be noted that the "speculative" claim about the relationship of God to Wisdom herself at the beginning of creation is not presented for its own sake but as backing for Wisdom's invitation with which the chapter concludes. It is because of Wisdom's intimate connection with the creator that she can claim, "He who finds me finds life and obtains favor from the Lord" (Prov. 8:35).

Nonetheless the theological backing for the invitation moves us very far from any sense that Old Testament wisdom is to be equated with the best of human insight or even the accumulated experience of the community of the wise. Paul Ricoeur helps us on this score.

> Nothing is further from the spirit of the sages than the idea of an automony of thinking, a humanism of the good life; in short, of a wisdom in the Stoic or Epicurean mode founded on the self-sufficiency of thought. This is why wisdom is held to be a gift of God in distinction from the "knowledge of good

and evil" promised by the Serpent. What is more, for the scribes following the Exile, Wisdom was personified into a transcendent feminine figure . . . She lives with God and she has accompanied creation from its very beginning. Intimacy with Wisdom is not to be distinguished from intimacy with God.[15]

Scott suggests the direction of thought which leads the writers of Proverbs to the claim that Wisdom is a divine reality which was present from the beginning of creation. Taking a clue from the fundamental claim of the Book of Proverbs, that "the fear of the Lord is the beginning of knowledge" (Prov. 1:7), the writer now suggests that Wisdom "is the beginning in a much more radical sense—as the first principle of the cosmic order, associated with Yahweh himself in its creation."[16]

It is clear here that Wisdom is not directly identified with the creator, and it is not clear that the Wisdom presented in Proverbs 8 can rightly be described as herself "divine." What is clear is that Wisdom is now represented as having a reality which is separate from the reality of the created world. Wisdom is not simply the ability to perceive the nature of worldly phenomena nor the orders which regulate phenomena. Nor is Wisdom identified simply with the regularities of creation themselves. Now Wisdom is a principle of order and significance which precedes creation. By implication, at least, Wisdom is a lesser partner in the activity of the creator, and what God creates, God creates according to the blueprints and purposes which Wisdom represents.[17]

It would probably be a mistake to see in this personification of Wisdom a thoroughly developed "metaphysical" scheme. What we can see is that, according to Proverbs and Job 28 at least, the wisdom of the wise men is set in a strongly theological framework. At its best, human knowledge, which starts with the fear of God, leads not only to an understanding of creation, but to reverence before God. Wisdom leads not only to an understanding of creation, but to reverence before God the creator. The best that human knowledge can do is radically limited before the wise purposes of God, which transcend all human knowledge and which preceded the creation itself.[18]

Therefore, though von Rad may push the paradox further than it need go, he certainly points to the tension—or the rich dialectic—in wisdom literature as a whole:

One can, therefore, only warn against trying to see the specific factor in wisdom simply as the manifestation of a rationality which was independent of faith. . . .
It was perhaps Israel's greatness that she did not keep faith and knowledge

apart. The experiences of the world were for her always divine experiences as well, and the experiences of God were for her experiences of the world.[19]

WISDOM MATERIAL IN THE NEW TESTAMENT

Though the New Testament contains no books which could be called "wisdom literature" in their entirety, nonetheless the influence of wisdom discourse is often evident as a background for certain New Testament passages, and at some points both the sayings of Jesus and the writings of Paul show features characteristic of wisdom literature. I have no intention of presenting a complete survey of such literature but want to look primarily at some specific passages which suggest wisdom literature's influence on the New Testament.

MATTHEW

The most pervasive use of wisdom motifs and of wisdom-like proverbial material among the gospels occurs in the Gospel of Matthew. Here Jesus' sayings (as in the parallel sayings in Luke) often show both the formal characteristics of wisdom discourse and something of the empirical and theological slant which we saw to be characteristic of wisdom literature. More than that, there are clues in Matthew's gospel that Matthew sees Jesus himself as a figure of personified wisdom, one who calls people to himself as does Wisdom in Proverbs 8.

The Gospel of Matthew is strikingly different, however, from the Book of Proverbs or Ecclesiastes (and more like Job) in that the proverbial material is contained within the larger context of that gospel. This means that the identity of the "wise man" is far more essential to the authority and meaning of the proverbs than in the traditional identification of the wise men of Proverbs or Ecclesiastes with King Solomon. The proverbs presented may be self-evidently true, but their claim to truth derives ultimately from the fact that they are proverbs of Jesus.

Furthermore, the whole gospel setting—particularly in Matthew—presupposes a fundamental apocalyptic or at least eschatological framework which is strikingly different from Proverbs or Ecclesiastes. Both Proverbs and Ecclesiastes assume, either implicitly or explicitly, that the world will continue to follow regular patterns without radical change or interruption. Matthew's eschatological outlook, on the other hand, assumes that in Jesus' ministry the prophesied kingdom of Heaven begins to impinge upon human history and that in the foreseeable future the shape of history will be radically altered by the coming of the Son of Man in glory (see especially Matthew 25). Therefore the ability of Wisdom to talk about the way the world goes is qualified by the constant reminder that the world will not go that way for long.[20]

A typical instance of Jesus' "wisdom" sayings in Matthew is Matthew 6:24: "No one can serve two masters; for either he will hate the one and love the other, or he will be devoted to one and despise the other. You cannot serve God and mammon." The proverbial "center" of the saying is a typical example of wisdom discourse. In form it demonstrates *antithetical parallelism.*[21] In context it does not pretend to be a word of revelation from God but an observation of the way the world goes: "It is, in fact, impossible for anyone to serve two masters. Look around you at those who attempt it, and see for yourself." Again the style is not imperative but descriptive, and even the closing "point" is presented as a statement of the case rather than as a command: "Serve God and not Mammon." (The parallel is Luke 16:13.)

Matt. 6:27 does not include the proverbial form of parallelism, but its rhetorical question relies again on common sense and on the assumption that the hearer can look at the world around and discover the truth of the claim: "Which of you by being anxious can add one cubit to his span of life?" The style is rather more like Ecclesiastes than Proverbs. "The more words, the more vanity, and what is man the better?" (Eccl. 6:11).

Matt. 6:28–29, like much wisdom material, draws a lesson from the "order of nature" which is appropriate to the social or human order. "Consider the lilies of the field, how they grow; they neither toil nor spin; yet I tell you, even Solomon in all his glory was not arrayed like one of these." Jesus then goes on to draw the moral from the proverb, which in some ways was clear enough by itself. "But if God so clothes the grass of the field which today is alive and tomorrow is thrown into the oven, will he not much more clothe you, O men of little faith?" (Matt. 6:30). Here the appeal is both to God as creator and sustainer and to the regular order of events which God sustains.[22]

The proverbs of Matt. 6:34 are brief enough to serve as self-contained aphorisms. Both of them rely on observation, common sense; both of them perhaps suggest an acknowledgment of the regular orders of life. Further, there is an acknowledgment of the limits of what one's planning or one's wisdom can accomplish.

"Therefore do not be anxious about tomorrow
  For tomorrow will be anxious about itself."
"Let the day's own trouble be sufficient for the day."

The former proverb is strikingly similar to Prov. 27:1 in its sense both of

the orderly distinction between today and tomorrow and of the limits of
human knowledge:

> Do not boast about tomorrow,
>   for you do not know what a day may bring forth.

Not only does Jesus act as a kind of "wisdom" teacher within Matthew's
gospel but there are also at least two instances where he seems to represent
Wisdom personified, the one who invites people to learn from him and to
obey him, and the one in whose teachings the wise will find life.

When Jesus concludes the Sermon on the Mount (the source of the
"wisdom" sayings we have cited), he tells the story of the wise and foolish
builders:

> "Every one then who hears these words of mine and does them will be like
> a wise man who built his house upon the rock; and the rain fell, and the floods
> came, and the winds blew and beat upon that house, but it did not fall,
> because it had been founded upon the rock. And every one who hears these
> words of mine and does not do them will be like a foolish man who built his
> house upon the sand; and the rain fell, and the floods came, and the winds
> blew and beat against that house, and it fell; and great was the fall of it"
> (Matt. 7:24–27).[23]

While the specific vocabulary here is not precisely the same as that in
Proverbs 1:20–33 (in the Septuagint version), the idea of Wisdom calling
people to trust in her and warning them of dire consequences if they do not
is strikingly similar.

> Wisdom cries aloud in the street;
>   in the markets she raises her voice; . . .
> Because I have called and you refused to listen . . .
> I also will laugh at your calamity;
>   I will mock when panic strikes you,
> when panic strikes you like a storm, . . .
> For the simple are killed by their turning away,
>   and the complacence of fools destroys them;
> but he who listens to me will dwell secure,
>   and will be at ease, without dread of evil.

Even more clearly, many commentators have seen that in Matthew
11:28–30 Jesus echoes the voice of personified Wisdom, especially as we
find it represented in the "intertestamental" book of the *Wisdom of Sirach
(Ecclesiasticus).*[24]

> "Come to me, all who labor and are heavy laden, and I will give you rest.
> Take my yoke upon you, and learn from me, for I am gentle and lowly in
> heart, and you will find rest for your souls. For my yoke is easy and my burden
> is light" (Matt. 11:28–30).

Wisdom will praise herself,
  and will glory in the midst of her people. . . .
"Come to me, you who desire me,
  and eat your fill of my produce.
For the remembrance of me is sweeter than honey,
  and my inheritance sweeter than the honeycomb.
Those who eat me will hunger for more,
  and those who drink me will thirst for more.
Whoever obeys me will not be put to shame,
  and those who work with my help will not sin" (Sir. 24:1–22).

(The invitation to "eat" and "drink" of wisdom recall Jesus' discourses on living water in John 4 and bread from heaven in John 6. Though the Jesus of John's gospel is not himself a speaker of proverbial wisdom, he may represent something of God's eternal wisdom—now called the Logos—personified, or incarnate.)

No one would claim that any of the gospels presents Jesus primarily as a teacher of wisdom, or that wisdom discourse was central to Jesus' ministry, insofar as we can reconstruct the elements of that ministry. Nonetheless, there are places, especially in the Gospel of Matthew, where Jesus clearly is presented as a great teacher of wisdom (though always more than that). There are sayings which are strikingly like sayings from wisdom literature such as the Proverbs, though these are often qualified and placed in an eschatological setting. There are indications in both Matthew and John that qualities elsewhere attributed to personified Wisdom are now attributed to Jesus. *He* is the one who knows the Father and who brings true wisdom to those who will heed his voice.

PAUL

In the writings of Paul, too, it is possible to discern certain motifs and arguments and sayings which seem typical of wisdom literature and its perspective. Once again, however, the use of wisdom material is qualified by the larger eschatological context. Paul looks to the fulfillment of the eschatological promise, when God will be all in all (cf. 1 Cor. 15:28; Rom. 8:18–25). At the same time Paul maintains that the eschatological fulfillment has already begun in the cross and resurrection of Jesus. Therefore, the life of the believer is already marked by the gift of God's spirit and by the new direction and possibility which the spirit provides (cf. Rom. 8:1–11; Gal. 5:1–25).

Within this larger framework of eschatological gift and expectation, however, Paul still pays attention to the ongoing orders of life which are qualified but not totally abolished by the new age which has begun. There are several ways in which Paul makes use of wisdom motifs and sayings.

Sometimes Paul uses proverbial material, probably drawn from popular discourse, *to strengthen a point* he wants to make. Twice he uses the proverb "A little leaven leavens the whole lump" to warn Christians about the presence of harmful persons within their congregation. (The proverb functions rather like our popular "one rotten apple spoils the barrel.") In 1 Cor. 5:6, Paul is urging the church to discipline a man engaged in incestuous behavior. In Gal. 5:9, he is warning the Galatians against those believers who would insist that Gentile Christians should be circumcised while Paul maintains that laws regarding circumcision are not binding on Christians—ones who are justified by faith.[25]

Another proverb appears twice in the Pauline letters, in slightly different forms. The typical parallelism of biblical proverbs is maintained in 2 Cor. 9:6, where Paul is encouraging the Corinthians to give generously in the offering for the Jerusalem poor.

> He who sows sparingly will also reap sparingly,
> and he who sows bountifully will also reap bountifully.

In Gal. 6:7, the proverb is a simple one-line aphorism, though it is qualified by the theological warning, "God is not mocked, for whatever a man sows, that he will also reap." Here the question is not the specific issue of the offering but rather a reminder of the significance and consequences of the fundamental decision whether to live according to the standards of this world (the flesh) or according to the standards of God (the Spirit.)[26]

Though Paul uses these proverbs in various ways and, as we shall see, often qualifies them by other claims and concerns, they do show characteristics typical of the appeal to wisdom. Both the saying about the leaven and the saying about sowing and reaping are based on observation of the world; they are therefore empirical. Each of them—especially the proverb about sowing and reaping—depends on a view of the orderly nature of creation. It is a rule that sparse sowing yields sparse reaping. Both of them represent "common sense," both because they represent ordinary, good sense, and because they appeal to popular, shared knowledge. Indeed, it seems unlikely that Paul coined either proverb and far more likely that in each case he used the proverb precisely as an appeal to common knowledge, and perhaps as a proverb his readers would already know and affirm.

In another instance, 1 Cor. 8:1, Paul more likely coins the "proverb" himself. In criticizing the Corinthians' excessive stress on the importance of knowledge (*gnōsis*), he writes the following reminder, in typical proverbial style:

"Knowledge" puffs up,
but love builds up.

(The Greek does not have the obvious word-play of the RSV translation.) Here, as in so many proverbs, the warning is presented not as an imperative, but as a descriptive aphorism. Again it is based on empirical observation, but now not on observation and comparison within the "natural" order, but on observation of the social order. This is how love and knowledge work within human communities (particularly the community of the church).

Paul does not simply use wisdom material and wisdom-like arguments in his letters, he also *deepens and qualifies proverbial material* by placing it within his larger theological concerns. For example, in Rom. 12:20 he quotes quite directly from Prov. 25:21–22, and includes even the somewhat cryptic sanction for loving the enemy which is found in Proverbs: "'If your enemy is hungry, feed him; if he is thirsty, give him drink; for by so doing you will heap burning coals upon his head.'" The larger context for this proverbial wisdom is set within Rom. 12:2, which does not appeal to the orders of this world but to the new orders of the eschatological age. "Do not be conformed to this world but be transformed by the renewal of your mind, that you may prove what is the will of God, what is good and acceptable and perfect." The immediate context for the quotation from Proverbs is set with the remainder of the coming judgment: "Beloved, never avenge yourselves, but leave it to the wrath of God; for it is written, 'Vengeance is mine, I will repay, says the Lord'" (Rom. 12:19).

At other points Paul adds to the "common sense" warnings and sanctions of wisdom those further sanctions and reasons which seem appropriate to his sense that a new age has dawned in Christ. So, for instance, 1 Cor. 5:6 dealing with the incestuous man begins simply with the proverbial reminder but moves to a more specifically christological claim:

Do you not know that a little leaven leavens the whole lump? Cleanse out the old leaven that you may be a new lump, as you really are unleavened. For Christ, our paschal lamb, has been sacrificed. Let us, therefore, celebrate the festival, not with the old leaven, the leaven of malice and evil, but with the unleavened bread of sincerity and truth (1 Cor. 5:6–8).

Here Paul argues that the Corinthians live with a new situation brought about by the death of Christ, and that therefore it is inappropriate and impossible for them to live according to their old, "leavened" ways.

Gal. 6:7, as we have seen, qualifies the proverb "Whatever a man sows, that he will also reap" by a warning of judgment: "God is not mocked." And Paul's "reaping" is not simply the reaping of which typical wisdom might speak—the reaping of benefits within the orders of daily, social life. It is rather that reaping which comes in the judgment and mercy of God.

> For he who sows to his own flesh will from the flesh reap corruption; but he who sows to the Spirit will from the Spirit reap eternal life. And let us not grow weary in well-doing, for in due season we shall reap, if we do not lose heart (Gal. 6:8–9).

There is a further way in which Paul relates wisdom concerns to his larger eschatological framework. At some points *he uses arguments and phrases typical of wisdom literature to qualify what he thinks to be too enthusiastic and single-minded eschatological understanding.* This is particularly clear in the first letter to the Corinthians. Apparently the Corinthians have taken Paul's own claim that the eschatological age is breaking in in Jesus Christ, releasing believers from the bonds of the law and sin, and they have misinterpreted Paul to mean by that claim that for Christians, anything goes. Paul needs to qualify their enthusiastic embrace of the new age with the reminder that some of the conditions of creation and mortality are still valid. In 1 Cor. 6:12, Paul "creates" two proverbs. In each case it seems rather likely that the first line of the proverb, "all things are lawful," is a quotation from the Corinthians' letter to Paul. It may be, further, that in using this phrase, the Corinthians themselves are only quoting something Paul has told them in his earlier preaching. So Paul here qualifies, but does not deny, aphorisms of the Corinthian church which may originally have been his own:

> "All things are lawful for me,"
>   but not all things are helpful.
> "All things are lawful for me,"
>   but I will not be enslaved by anything (1 Cor. 6:12).

What is particularly interesting here is that Paul qualifies a kind of thoroughgoing reliance on "realized" eschatology and the gifts of the new age with reminders which are prudential, common-sensical, and in that way more appropriate to typical "wisdom" claims and sanctions. The further argument of the paragraph takes place in largely eschatological terms, but here there is the simple and straightforward "prudential" reminder that whatever may be legal, not everything is helpful, and that helpfulness is a legitimate ground on which to judge the faithful life.

Finally, *Paul also stresses the limits of human wisdom or human knowledge.* In 1 Cor. 8:2 we find the fairly typical "wisdom" claim that those who think themselves to be wise show by that very fact that they are not so wise as they think. Then Paul in his own way reminds the Corinthians that the fear of God is the beginning of wisdom by stressing the fundamental duty of the believer to love God and suggesting that true knowledge is not human knowledge of God but God's knowledge of humankind. The antithetical style itself suggests a wisdom proverb.

> If any one imagines that he knows something, he does not yet know as he ought to know. But if one loves God, one is known by him (1 Cor. 8:2,3).

In 1 Cor. 1:18–25, Paul qualifies the worth of wisdom by the claim that God has redeemed the world, not through wisdom, but through the foolishness of the cross. Explicitly it is the "Greek" quest for wisdom which Paul here criticizes, but certainly a severe limitation is placed on any sort of human wisdom in the light of the Messiah's crucifixion. We notice here that it is no longer simply the utter unsearchability of God's ways which casts doubt upon human wisdom. It is rather that now, in Jesus Christ (the Messiah), God's ways are known, but that the God who is known is known to have acted contrary to any human calculations or expectations.

In Rom. 11:33–36, Paul concludes a discussion of God's plan to include both Gentiles and Jews within God's final redemption of the world. On the one hand, Paul claims to have knowledge (through study of Scripture) of the way in which God has determined this final redemption. On the other hand, he wants to claim that such knowledge is always beyond human understanding and can only be given by God.

> O the depth of the riches and wisdom and knowledge of God!
>   How unsearchable are his judgments and how inscrutable
>   his ways!
> "For who has known the mind of the Lord,
>   or who has been his counselor?"
> "Or who has given a gift to him
>   that he might be repaid?" (Note here that Paul quotes
>   Isa. 40:13 and Job 35:7.)
> For from him and through him and to him are all things. To him be glory for ever. Amen.

Here, as in Job 28, true wisdom is seen to be a property of God alone, and the proper human response is not so much knowledge as reverence before that wisdom which transcends our knowing.

As with the gospels it is clear that Paul's letters are not primarily examples of "wisdom" literature. Within the larger eschatological and christological framework, however, wisdom motifs do emerge, and sometimes Paul quotes or invents typical wisdom proverbs.

Paul is quite capable of underlining an exhortation or criticizing the behavior of some believers by appealing to common sense—to empirical observation and to the shared wisdom of humankind. He also can take such wisdom and qualify and deepen its implication in the light of the new work of God in Jesus Christ. Paul can appeal to the orders of nature and of society, but he also wishes to insist that in Jesus Christ, God is making a new creation. Because Paul's churches live already under the fulfillment of the cross and resurrection, the regular orders of society can never be sufficient guide for their conduct. But because the kingdoms of this world have not yet become altogether the kingdoms of God, human orders and human sense can provide some guidance for faithful behavior.

Finally, as with the Old Testament writers, Paul insists that human wisdom is radically limited before the ultimate wisdom of the counsels of God. Because of the cross, Paul is acutely aware that God can make the most lofty human wisdom seem foolish before God's own surprising purposes.

DEALING WITH WISDOM LITERATURE TODAY

The characteristic features which we have discerned in describing wisdom literature give some clues to the ways in which wisdom material may be used authoritatively today.

WISDOM AND EXPERIENCE

One of the fundamental appeals of wisdom literature is the appeal to experience. Implicitly the proverb or the saying tells us, "Look around you. Isn't this the way it is?" Where prophecy appeals to oracles received from God and narrative appeals to those moments when God acts surprisingly in the world, wisdom appeals to what the discerning person can see if he or she simply looks around. If the proverb says that "A soft answer turns away wrath, but a harsh word stirs up anger" (Prov. 15:1), we need not assume that the proverb represents a divine proclamation to test its validity. We need only look around to see that it is true. When Jesus says, "No man can serve two masters," we can test the truth of his observation by observing lives, perhaps our own life, caught in the impossible task of trying to hold onto competing loyalties with equal devotion.

Wisdom literature not only appeals to familiar experience but allows us to see the world around us more clearly, more freshly. The comparison of a clever proverb causes us to say, "Of course, that is exactly how the world is. I'd never thought of it in precisely that way before, but I can see exactly what you mean." When Paul says, "A little leaven leavens the whole loaf," and draws the implication, "One immoral believer can ruin the whole community," the Corinthian readers are supposed to say, "Ah, he's right about the leaven, and how apt is the comparison." When the writer of Ecclesiastes describes the world he sees, he describes what everyone can see, but he observes it so carefully that we are forced to understand what we have seen:

> Again, I saw vanity under the sun: a person who has no one, either son or brother, yet there is no end to all his toil, and his eyes are never satisfied with riches, so that he never asks, "For whom am I toiling and depriving myself of pleasure?" This also is vanity and an unhappy business (Eccl. 4:7–8).

Particularly in moral questions, Christians have a tendency to move automatically to concerns and warrants based on models of prophecy or narrative. We seek to rely on some direct word from God ("thus says the Lord"). Or we try to discern what God is doing in history and to act according to that perception.

Wisdom provides a more modest model, but a useful one for dealing with moral questions. Sometimes it is perfectly appropriate to make moral judgments on the basis of experience. How does the world go? What enriches human life, what destroys it? Proverbs argues against sexual relations with prostitutes, not because God has condemned such relations, but because a clear look at the world reveals that they produce nothing but trouble (e.g., Prov. 2:16–19). Paul argues against some of the practices of the Corinthian church, not only on the grounds that they violate the Word of God or the marks of the kingdom, but on the grounds that they are not helpful. And when he goes on to say, "All things are lawful for me, but I will not be enslaved by anything," that claim is based on his empirical observation that certain kinds of freedom turn into the most debilitating kind of slavery. Habits and passions which we think are marks of our freedom can soon hold us in their thrall (1 Cor. 6:12).

Sometimes in dealing with moral decisions the church would do well to look carefully at the world around. What does help? What is useful? What frees? What enslaves? Appeals to such ordinary experience are not unfaithful; in their own way they are as appropriate as appeals to the oracles of God, or to what God is doing in history.

WISDOM AND COMMON SENSE

Closely related to the understanding of wisdom as based in experience is the reminder that wisdom stresses the values of common sense. In part this means that wisdom literature appeals to our ordinary sense. Its validation does not depend on any special religious sensibilities. All that is required is that the "wise" person have eyes to see.

More than that, wisdom depends on common sense as *shared* sense—sense which is not the property of any one discerning individual but the property both of a community and of a tradition. We recall von Rad's description: "(In wisdom literature) knowledge does not accrue to an individual, nor even to a generation. It acquires its status and its binding claim only when it appears as the common possession of a nation or of a broad stratum within a nation."[27]

Old Testament wisdom literature clearly derives in its present form from a "school" of sages who passed on, shared, modified, collected that wisdom which they had inherited from the generations before them. This legacy has two implications for the present authority of wisdom discourse or of "wisdom-like" material within the church.

First, in matters of empirical discernment and moral judgment, the sharing of insights and observations is essential. In dealing with precisely the kinds of issues that wisdom literature deals with—sexual mores, business practices, the relationship between righteousness and wealth, the relationship between freedom and responsibility—the individual is not called upon simply to base all decisions on his or her own observation. These are issues where common, shared sense is vital. The church can provide that context in which people think together. It need not always be the case that we try to work out the issues of the moral and faithful life by appealing to direct oracles of God and deciding who is a true and false prophet. Sometimes we can more appropriately share our observations of the world. What builds up and what only puffs up? Where is freedom helpful and where is it not? What implications do particular ethical strategies involve?

Second, in matters of empirical discernment and moral judgment, we need to pay attention to common sense, not only that wisdom we share with our contemporaries but that wisdom which we inherit from our ancestors.

Scott emphasizes this element of wisdom's influence:

> The first point to be made is that it is not common sense to begin the search for modern solutions by wiping the slate clean of the accumulated wisdom of

> thoughtful observers of the human scene in the last 5,000 years. . . . Ancient
> Israel's wisdom is at the very least one significant component of man's
> knowledge of himself. With such knowledge he must begin if he is to
> envisage realistically the social goals toward which he strives.[28]

This does not mean that we can see the world exactly as our ancestors saw
it. What we see is determined in part by contexts which they simply did
not share. When we look at human actions we have categories based on
contemporary psychological analysis which our forebears lacked. When
we look at political activity we have more explicit theories for linking
political decisions to economic interests than did the writers of wisdom
literature. Yet the observations of the wise men and of Paul and of other
discerning people throughout history become part of the material for our
reflection. We do not observe or decide in isolation either from our
contemporaries or from our forebears.

THE LIMITS OF WISDOM

In its contemporary reflection and action the church needs to acknowledge that neither wisdom literature nor our own best wisdom can provide
a sufficient foundation and guide.

To say so is in part to acknowledge a limitation which we can perceive as
students of wisdom discourse. Insofar as wisdom literature depends
precisely upon "common sense" it runs the danger of being insufficiently
sensitive to the novel. Wisdom is based upon the shared understandings
both of a community and a tradition. Experience, however, sometimes
refuses to fit into the mold of the expected or the traditional. Every faithful
Christian person and every faithful Christian community will need to
acknowledge those moments when "what we all know" is not knowledge
enough, and "the way it's always been done" is simply not the way to do it.
Von Rad acknowledges this limitation in wisdom literature:

> But precisely in its quality as a communal possession this knowledge finds
> itself on dangerous ground. Certainly, on the basis of a long period of trial, it
> can make for itself a claim to stability and validity. But, insofar as it becomes
> the possession of all, it is in danger of simplifying and generalizing truths
> which can be generalized only to a certain extent.[29]

When Paul argues in 1 Corinthians 1 that God has made foolish the
wisdom of the world in the cross of Christ, he is arguing in part that it is
precisely the novel, the unexpected, for which wisdom cannot account.
For Christians, therefore, the cross serves always as a reminder that the
best calculation based on our ongoing experience will sometimes be
challenged by novel events, unexpected experiences, and surprising

outcomes. Tradition and wisdom always stand under question in face of surprise.

In part the acknowledgement of the limitations of wisdom does not come from outside wisdom literature, but from within wisdom discourse itself. We have noted that traditionally, wisdom literature acknowledges that human wisdom is limited by the deeper wisdom and unsearchable purposes of God. Wisdom literature itself calls upon faithful people to exercise their minds and their common understandings with a necessary humility. According to wisdom literature, Christians should not be surprised when the best laid plans of people go askew. "The horse is made ready for the day of battle, but the victory belongs to the Lord" (Prov. 21:31). And according to wisdom literature, faithful people should acknowledge that beyond the boundaries of our deepest wisdom and most perceptive observation lie realms of mystery which are forever hidden within the deeper wisdom of God.

> "But where shall wisdom be found?
>   And where is the place of understanding?
> Man does not know the way to it,
>   and it is not found in the land of the living."
> "God understands the way to it,
>   and he knows the place.
> For he looks to the ends of the earth,
>   and sees everything under the heavens" (Job 28:12, 23–24).

Wisdom literature itself, therefore, suggests two appropriate elements for the contemporary search for understanding. It validates the use of human knowledge—common sense—in our observations and our actions. It recalls us to a necessary humility in any appeal to our knowledge or common sense. The most we can know is not very much compared to the deeper wisdom of God. The best we can do may turn out very differently from the way that we had planned. When we turn to the authority of wisdom in our churches we are encouraged to use our minds and discouraged from deifying them.

WISDOM AND FAITH

This brings us to make explicit what is implicit in much of what we have said about the contemporary authority of wisdom. At least in their present canonical form, wisdom books and wisdom sayings have central theological implications. (The implications of Ecclesiastes, as we have seen, are rather different from those of the other literature.) Rightly to acknowledge the authority of wisdom literature is not only to acknowledge the appropriateness of human intellect and experience, it is also to acknowledge the validity of certain claims about God.

For one thing, certainly in Proverbs 8, Wisdom herself is especially related to creation and to that order of phenomena which transcends the phenomena themselves. In Proverbs 8, Wisdom is not identified with the creation so much as it is seen to be a co-worker with the Creator.

Wisdom literature suggests that it is perfectly appropriate for faithful people to seek to understand the orders and regularities of the world, but it further suggests that rightly to understand those orders and regularities is to perceive them as provided and sustained by God the Creator. Wisdom is therefore not separate from faithfulness, because wisdom rightly exercised points us beyond observation of the way of the world to celebration of the ways of God.

We can make this claim somewhat differently. Wisdom literature sets its observations about human knowledge within the fundamental claim about the first principle of proper human behavior:

> The fear of the LORD is the beginning of knowledge;
>   fools despise wisdom and instruction. (Prov. 1:7)
> And (God) said to man,
> "Behold, the fear of the Lord, that is wisdom;
>   and to depart from evil is understanding" (Job 28:28).

That is to say, we have mistaken the proper use of wisdom if wisdom causes us to turn from reverence for God to reverence for our own abilities and discoveries. The authority of wisdom is always a modest authority within the Christian life; wisdom literature itself suggests that wisdom is bracketed by the acknowledgement that God created the orders of the world and that God transcends the orders of the world. The deepest searches of human wisdom are qualified and enriched by reverence before what we do not know and trust in the one who transcends our knowledge.

All this is to say, in the most concrete terms, that in the contemporary life of Christians and of the church, the search for wisdom is still qualified by the need for prayer. When we have looked most carefully at the world around us, discussed most diligently with our fellows what our common experience would suggest, discerned those orders which lead us to understand the consequences of our action, still we do not know enough. God's purpose contains more than our wisdom can discover, and God's activity is often apt to surprise. Beyond the strategies of discovery and discernment there is the need for humility and prayer.

Moral discourse among faithful people in our day might be radically altered *if* more often we admitted that we do not know for sure. Our best observations suggest what we ought to do, but we constantly subject our best guesses to the possibility of surprise, and conduct our moral arguments under the discipline of prayer.

WISDOM IN LARGER CONTEXTS

The whole pattern of this book reminds us that *no single model* for understanding Scripture's authority nor our own lives will suffice. Those who gathered the canon of the Old Testament through the ages included the wisdom literature, but preceded it both with prophetic material and with narrative and law (in the Hebrew Bible's order). The compilers of the various wisdom books, as we have seen, are themselves concerned to qualify the stress on wisdom with the larger and more fundamental insistence on faithfulness and piety.

Both the gospels and epistles, Paul's especially, use considerable amounts of "wisdom" or "wisdom-like" material, but it is clear that in neither case is wisdom the fundamental guide to God's activity or the human response. In both Matthew and Paul, for instance, appeals to wisdom are radically qualified by the sense that faithful people live within the expectation of God's kingdom, and that our lives are qualified not only by the way the world goes but by what the kingdom is and is to be. For Matthew and Paul the clearest guide to the transcendent purposes of God is not that wisdom which existed before human history, but Jesus Christ present in human history.

For Matthew the guide to God's purposes in the past is more apt to be prophecy than the sense of the regularity of human orders, and Jesus comes as the fulfillment, not of the expectations of the wise, but of the proclamations of the prophets. For Paul the foolishness of the cross, by providing precisely what the wise could not expect, throws into question even the best of human calculation and the most acceptable of traditional knowledge.

Nonetheless, within the larger frameworks of the biblical canon and the larger theological concerns of writers like Matthew and Paul, wisdom clearly has its place. It may be a modest place, but often the decisions of the day are modest decisions. So today, within the reflection of the church, there is room not only for that faith which listens to the Word of God and that discernment which seeks God's surprising activity in history. There is also room for common sense, looking at the way the world goes, sharing experience with one another, making our best guess as to what we should do and what effects our action will have. Christians will always want to use their best judgment humbly and prayerfully, but the place of wisdom in the canon suggests that it is perfectly appropriate for Christians to use their best judgment, and that thoughtfulness and faithfulness may sometimes complement each other in the purposes of God.

NOTES

1. For Paul Ricoeur's discussion of wisdom literature, cf. "Toward a Hermeneutic of the Idea of Revelation," in *Essays on Biblical Interpretation,* ed. Lewis S. Mudge (Philadelphia: Fortress Press, 1980), 85–88.

2. We shall be dealing primarily with Proverbs and Ecclesiastes in looking at the Old Testament material, since we have already discussed the Book of Job as an instance of biblical narrative. The category "wisdom," it will be noted, is less a description of genre than it is of content, and while Job's form is that of poetic narrative, some of the arguments contained therein show close affinities to the wisdom school.

3. For a discussion of the subject, cf. Gerhard von Rad, *Wisdom in Israel* (Nashville: Abingdon Press, 1972), 15–23; and R. B. Y. Scott, *The Way of Wisdom* (New York: Macmillan, 1971), 1–2, 23–47.

4. Cf. von Rad, *Wisdom in Israel,* 296–97.

5. One recalls Thomas Gray, "Where ignorance is bliss,/'tis folly to be wise" ("Ode on a Distant Prospect of Eton College," line 91), except that for Ecclesiastes ignorance is not bliss, either.

6. For a discussion of this issue, see Wayne Sibley Towner, "The Renewed Authority of Old Testament Wisdom for Contemporary Faith," in George W. Coats and Burke O. Long, eds. *Canon and Authority: Essays in Old Testament Religion and Theology* (Philadelphia: Fortress Press, 1977), 132–47. Towner defines "secular" in a careful, rather technical way so as to clarify the discussion. Secularity is not a-theistic here, but rather operates without any "assumption of immediate divine casuality," 132.

7. Scott, *The Way of Wisdom,* 113.

8. Von Rad, *Wisdom in Israel,* 35.

9. For the contrast between "wisdom" and contemporary versions of "reason," see von Rad, *Wisdom in Israel,* 296–98.

10. Von Rad, *Wisdom in Israel,* 3–4.

11. Von Rad, *Wisdom in Israel,* 31. For a very helpful discussion of the style of wisdom, see the entire chapter on pages 24–50.

12. Whether the more "theological" elements represent a later development in the stream of wisdom understanding is a question I am not qualified to adjudicate. For discussion, cf. von Rad, *Wisdom in Israel,* 104 and Brevard Childs, *Introduction to the Old Testament as Scripture* (Philadelphia: Fortress Press, 1979), 556–59.

13. Von Rad, *Wisdom in Israel,* 106; for some questions about the dialectic, cf. Towner, "Renewed Authority," 136, 140–41.

14. It seems likely that this theological elaboration is a rather late development in wisdom discourse, though dating such matters is notoriously difficult. Certainly

it represents something of an understandable development from the other theological implications of the wisdom literature which we have been discussing.

15. Ricoeur, "Toward a Hermeneutic," 88.

16. Scott, *The Way of Wisdom*, 84.

17. Cf. von Rad, *Wisdom in Israel*, 171–72.

18. "Wisdom speculation," which presents wisdom as a personified figure, is also found in the "intertestamental" book of Sirach (Ecclesiasticus), chap. 24 and elsewhere. It may well be that some understanding of a personified wisdom which was with God at the creation played into the claims of the prologue of the Gospel of John concerning the Word which was with God at the beginning, and through which everything was created.

19. Von Rad, *Wisdom in Israel*, 61–62.

20. Cf. William A. Beardslee, *Literary Criticism of the New Testament* (Philadelphia: Fortress Press, 1970), 39, for the reminder that these sayings and any pre-gospel collections of sayings *now* find their meaning within the larger context of the gospels themselves.

21. Beardslee, *Literary Criticism*, 35–36, 39.

22. For a close parallel in style and in the use of comparison, cf. Prov. 6:6–9, which begins, "Go to the ant, O sluggard; consider her ways, and be wise. Without having any chief, officer or ruler, she prepares her food in summer, and gathers her sustenance in harvest. How long will you lie there, O sluggard? When will you arise from your sleep?" And then a parallel proverb draws the moral: "A little sleep, a little slumber, a little folding of the hands to rest, and poverty will come upon you like a vagabond, and want like an armed man" (Prov. 6:6–11).

23. Cf. Prov. 14:1.

24. Beardslee, *Literary Criticism*, 35.

25. On the Galatians passage as an instance of a wisdom proverb., cf. Hans Dieter Betz, *Galatians: A Commentary on Paul's Letter to the Churches at Galatia*, Hermeneia: A Historical-Critical Commentary on the Bible (Philadelphia: Fortress Press, 1979), 266.

26. Again on the wisdom nature of the Galatians passage, cf. Betz, *Galatians*, 307.

27. Von Rad, *Wisdom in Israel*, 3.

28. Scott, *The Way of Wisdom*, 225.

29. Von Rad, *Wisdom in Israel*, 3–4.

5 / The Authority of Witness

The final variety of biblical literature to be discussed is what I call the literature of witness. Strictly speaking this is not a separate literary type, but rather represents an aspect of various and diverse biblical works.[1] Furthermore the amount of literature which can be characterized as literature of witness comprises only a relatively small part of the Bible, and no book in its entirety represents this kind of literature.

THE NATURE OF THE LITERATURE OF WITNESS

The concept of the witness is derived primarily from the language of the courtroom.[2] Perhaps we can best recall the nature of "witnessing" by constructing the role of the witness in a courtroom scene.

The purpose of witnessing is fundamentally to convince, to make a case. In the traditional American trial, the purpose of witnessing is to convince a jury. The lawyer for the defense, for example, calls a witness to the stand and evokes from that witness testimony which helps the jury to decide the outcome of the case.

To be valid, the testimony must be based on the experience of the witness: "This is what I have heard, this is what I have seen." The value we place on the direct experience of the witness is reflected in our phrase for the most persuasive kind of evidence: "eyewitness testimony." On the other hand, the argument presented to the jury is not simply self-evidently true. Evidence is presented on the assumption that the jury will finally be required to make a *decision*, to make a judgment, and that judgment will determine the outcome of the case.

The jury has the right to raise two rather different sorts of questions about the witness: (1) Is the testimony true? (2) Is the witness trustworthy? Any of us who have witnessed trial scenes in the movies, on television, or in person have seen both kinds of issues raised. On the one hand, clever lawyers seek to bring evidence to support or call into question the plausibility of a witness' claims. On the other hand, lawyers seek either to demonstrate or to question the witness' fundamental veracity. Is this the kind of person who usually can be trusted to tell the truth? Are there reasons why in this circumstance the witness might be protecting himself or herself at the expense of truth? Does the person's behavior show itself to be congruent with the testimony? (The person who claims to have had no knowledge of an illegal money-making scheme but who has opened a new bank account under a false name acts in such a way as to raise questions about his or her testimony.) Then, too, we have the device of the "character witness." The function of the character witness is not to help the jury decide whether a particular witness is correct in a particular testimony but to help the jury decide whether this is the kind of person whose testimony the jury can trust.

In the most dramatic cases, the witness is also the defendant. What is at stake in the testimony and in the jury's decision is fundamentally this: What do you think about this person? How do you decide this person's fate? If the jury decides that the witness speaks the truth and is trustworthy, then the witness is vindicated.

There is an extension of this close connection between the witness and his or her testimony in the fact that the Greek word *martus*, "witness," becomes the root of our word "martyr." Sometimes the way in which the witness shows his or her trustworthiness is in the willingness to suffer and even to die for those truths to which he or she testifies. Obviously the willingness to die for one's testimony does not prove in any conclusive way that the testimony is true, but it does lend credence to the claim that the one who testifies is trustworthy, to the claim that he or she believed this, and believed it deeply enough to die for it. So Joan of Arc's final refusal to recant suggests the depth of her belief in her voices and her mission; the martyrdom of Polycarp demonstrates the depth of his belief in Christ; the martyrdom of Jesus (where the Gethsemane story suggests the possibility of retreat) demonstrates the depth of his commitment to his cause.

Because of its stress both on testimony and on the one who testifies, the literature of witness in the Bible is by far closer to the modern genres of autobiography and confession than to other literature. On the whole those who write the biblical books or whose oracles and sayings are included in those books are quite reticent about disclosing details either of their own life or their own thought. Much of the literature is written anonymously, or *under* the authority and name of someone else. When we do have the name of the authors, or prophets, they are usually not concerned with presenting either their own experiences or their own reflections. In the Book of Amos, for instance, we have the record of the oracles Amos received from the Lord but no particular sense of what Amos thought about these oracles, or about his own prophetic task.[3] In the book of Luke-Acts, the author states briefly why he intends to write the books he writes, but he does not intervene in the literature to present his own opinions, or to demonstrate how the story he relates illumines his own experience, or to tell you what he himself was doing at the time of the events which he describes.[4]

Nonetheless there are some sections of biblical literature where the personality of the testifier does become part of the testimony, and here the interest of the reader shifts somewhat from an understanding of God's speaking or God's acting or of general human wisdom and focuses instead on the autobiography of the particular person and on the way in which who the person is relates to what the person says.

This focus on witness and testimony is particularly appropriate for the so-called confessions of Jeremiah and for the epistles of Paul, especially their more confessional sections.

THE CONFESSIONS OF JEREMIAH

Jeremiah's confessions[5] generally represent dialogues between the prophet and God.[6] The "audience" for the case which Jeremiah makes in his confession is God, and there is a sense in which Jeremiah tries to persuade God to vindicate him and to punish his enemies. In another sense, however, the fact that the confessions have now been written down and preserved suggests that they also represent testimony for future generations. Those around Jeremiah—Baruch and others—who have preserved this testimony suggest by that preservation that the confessions help to validate the prophet and the prophecy as well.

The way in which the confessions validate Jeremiah's role as prophet and his prophecies is by the congruity they show forth between the man's message and his life. Put as simply as possible, the congruity is this: the prophet is given the message of God's judgment on his people, judgment which will produce the greatest loss and sorrow. Yet the prophet does not stand apart from his prophecy. Not only will he participate in the loss and sorrow of his people but already his role as prophet brings loss and sorrow upon himself. That is to say, the prophet takes no delight in announcing suffering, since the suffering he announces falls first of all upon himself.

The congruity between the prophet's confessions and his larger mission is evident in yet another way. The ground of the prophet's complaint is precisely that the Lord has violated the very closeness of the divine relationship to the prophet by subjecting Jeremiah to such trials. The poignancy of the prophet's word to Israel is that the Lord who judges is the same Lord who has been in the closest personal relationship to this people.[7]

John Bright's description of the function of the confessions in Jeremiah misses this point:

> Few indeed are the men who could endure such treatment (the opposition even of his family and friends) with equanimity, and Jeremiah was certainly not among them. On the contrary, his spirit almost broke under it. He gave way to fits of angry recrimination, depression, and even suicidal despair. . . .
> That, of course, is not the whole of it. Were it so, we might put Jeremiah down as a weakling, a quitter, a small-spirited man whose faith was not great enough to endure the testing that was imposed upon it. And nothing could be farther from the truth. . . . He was driven by his calling to exhibit a strength that was not by nature his. More than this, Jeremiah seems himself to have understood that his complaints and recriminations were unworthy of him. . . . There is evidence that he struggled to purge himself of this weakness in his character.[8]

Yet as the confessions are presented in the Book of Jeremiah they are not evidence of a weakness which the prophet managed heroically to overcome; they are part and parcel of the prophet's office. The man who pronounces such woe, participates in the woe. In that sense Jeremiah is as good as his word: his life conforms to the judgment he pronounces. Gerhard von Rad is closer than Bright to the mark.

> Thus the reason why Baruch so conscientiously traces all the details of this *via dolorosa* is that the catastrophic events into which the prophet was drawn do not after all come by chance; instead, they bring the divine demolition to pass; here a human has in a unique fashion borne a part in the divine suffering.[9]

Though it is not always possible to connect Jeremiah's confessions directly with their historical setting, Jer. 12:1–6 apparently grows out of Jeremiah's realization of a plot to kill him by the men of Anathoth (cf. 11:21). Quite probably this is the plot to which the Lord's oracle refers in 12:6 where the plot is ascribed to Jeremiah's brothers and relatives.

> Righteous art thou, O LORD,
>   when I complain to thee;
>   yet I would plead my case before thee.
> Why does the way of the wicked prosper? (Jer. 12:1)

In Jeremiah's words to the Lord we can see quite explicitly the motifs of the trial which are appropriate to the literature of witness. Jeremiah argues his case before his jury and judge, the Lord. In part he seeks to persuade the

Lord to spare him and punish his enemies, but more centrally, Jeremiah seeks to argue the validity of his cause against the specious claims of his opponents. The key phrase here is one which raises precisely the question of integrity, of the congruity between the prophetic words and the prophetic experience:

"Thou art near in their mouth
   and far from their heart.
But Thou, O LORD, knowest me,
   thou seest me, and triest my mind toward thee" (Jer. 12:2b–3a).

Jeremiah is the one whose words and life both belong to the Lord; the Lord is near both Jeremiah's mouth and his heart.

The Lord's response gives no comfort. In effect it simply reminds the prophet that the prophetic task will continue to carry with it rejection and suffering. The prophet is not consoled; he is rather warned. What he has endured is just the beginning of what he must endure. " 'If you have raced with men on foot, and they have wearied you, how will you compete with horses?' " (Jer. 12:5). There is no escape from the fundamental suffering of the one who pronounces suffering for his people.[10]

Jeremiah 20 contains two confessions, of deepening despair (Jer. 20:7–13; 14–18).

Jer. 20:7–13 suggests a different sort of "trial" than the courtroom. Here the "trial" or "test" subjects the prophet to testing to see whether he will emerge worthily. Indeed the test which the Lord imposes is described in quite startling terms. The Lord is seen as an "agent provocateur" enticing the prophet into situations he would otherwise have avoided. In Jeremiah's complaint, "O Lord, thou hast deceived me, and I was deceived," the verb translated "deceived" really suggests seduction and violation[11] (Jer. 20:7). Jeremiah appeals to the Lord, "O Lord of hosts, who triest the righteous" (Jer. 20:12). The verb "try" is elsewhere used for testing or trying gold, as in Job 23:10.[12]

Again the text implies that the Lord serves as a judge, and again the prophet's case for himself rests on his claim to trustworthiness, to integrity. God will vindicate him because God sees not only his deeds but "the heart and the mind" (Jer. 20:12). God can therefore affirm the uprightness of Jeremiah's heart, his trustworthiness as a witness.

Jeremiah's trustworthiness as a witness is further underlined by the claim that, far from deriving either pleasure or gain from his prophetic role, Jeremiah suffers from his prophecy and actively seeks to discard the prophetic mantle. He is a prophet, not because he chooses to be a prophet, but because he is driven to prophecy:

> If I say, "I will not mention him,
>   or speak any more in his name,"
> there is in my heart as it were a burning fire
>   shut up in my bones,
> and I am weary with holding it in,
>   and I cannot (Jer. 20:9).

Again there is the clear sense that what Jeremiah's words proclaim Jeremiah's life embodies. The judgment which he pronounces on his people he feels most strongly upon himself. As the word of the Lord has become a reproach to Jeremiah's people, so, too, because of the mockery the prophet receives, the word of the Lord has brought reproach upon the prophet. He suffers as Israel will suffer because of the divine judgment which he himself pronounces.

Finally, however, Jeremiah's confidence is that the Lord will render a verdict favorable to himself and will enforce that verdict over against his enemies.

> But the LORD is with me as a dread warrior;
>   therefore my persecutors will stumble,
>   they will not overcome me. . . .
> O LORD of hosts, who triest the righteous,
>   who seest the heart and the mind,
> let me see thy vengeance upon them,
>   for to thee have I committed my cause (Jer. 20:11–12).

The concluding verses of the prophetic oracle are words of confidence and gratitude.

> Sing to the LORD:
>   praise the LORD!
> For he has delivered the life of the needy
>   from the hand of evildoers (Jer. 20:13).

In the final confession of Jeremiah, Jer. 20:14–18, that note of confidence has altogether disappeared. Now the prophetic role and the judgment Jeremiah must pronounce have become so thoroughly a burden and judgment for Jeremiah that he finds no comfort in hopes of final vindication.

> Cursed be the day
>   on which I was born!

The day when my mother bore me,
  let it not be blessed! . . .
Why did I come forth from the womb
  to see toil and sorrow
  and spend my days in shame?

Here the despair is almost unrelieved. As Jeremiah can sometimes pronounce the bitter judgment of the Lord on his people, so now Jeremiah feels most bitterly the pain of his own prophetic office. Though we have no way of knowing whether the confessions as we find them in the Book of Jeremiah represent the actual chronological order of their composition, as the book now stands Jeremiah experiences—in his final confession—an almost desperate darkness. Of course the book goes on to present numerous prophecies, of judgment and hope for Israel, but in the immediate context one senses that Jeremiah has become, even more than Israel, the victim of the divine word. There is no particular reflection on the meaning of suffering, no sense that God's purpose is hidden in the sorrow of the prophet. However, the later disciples who preserved this confession among the prophetic words must have wished to declare that the suffering of Jeremiah helped to vindicate his message. Far from invalidating the truth of his prophecy by showing him to be all too weak and human, the prophet's despair shows how fully he knew the judgment he pronounced and how totally that judgment was the product, not of his own delight in prophesying, but of the word which he was given to speak—even at the most incredible cost.

Finally, it is precisely Jeremiah's despair which enables the reader to see the congruity between the witness and his testimony, to confess that the man is as good as his word.

THE TESTIMONY OF PAUL

The very fact that Paul writes *letters* suggests that he is engaged in a form of testimony, of witness. The nature of the literature implies and requires a particularly close relationship between what is said and the person who says it. Prophetic oracles commonly begin: "Thus says the Lord," or "The word of the Lord . . ." The historical narratives of the Old Testament and the gospels of the New Testament are written and edited anonymously. The epistles, however, identify the writer, and their peculiar authority depends in part upon precisely that identification:

Paul, a servant of Jesus Christ, called to be an apostle, set apart for the gospel of God . . . To all God's beloved in Rome, who are called to be saints (Rom. 1:1, 7).

> Paul an apostle—not from men nor through man, but through Jesus Christ and God the Father, who raised him from the dead—and all the brethren who are with me, To the churches of Galatia (Gal. 1:1–2).

(It is a tribute to the particularly close relationship between author and authority that later pseudonymous letters—like 1 and 2 Timothy and Titus—sought to validate their arguments by using Paul's name as author and even by including "biographical" elements to lend credence to their claims.)

Moreover, as Robert Funk argues, Paul's letters serve as a substitute for his presence.[13] There are elements in the letters which indicate that Paul wishes he could be present, give the reasons why he cannot be present, and suggest that the letter itself is to be a substitute for his presence. The letter speaks for Paul, with his authority and in his place. In that sense it is inviolably connected with Paul as person and as apostle:

> . . . I wanted to come to you first, so that you might have a double pleasure; I wanted to visit you on my way to Macedonia, and to come back to you from Macedonia and have you send me on my way to Judea. Was I vacillating when I wanted to do this? Do I make my plans like a worldly man, ready to say Yes and No at once? As surely as God is faithful, our word to you has not been Yes and No. . . .
>
> But I call God to witness against me—it was to spare you that I refrained from coming to Corinth. Not that we lord it over your faith; we work with you for your joy, for you stand firm in your faith. For I made up my mind not to make you another painful visit. . . . For I wrote you out of much affliction and anguish of heart and with many tears, not to cause you pain but to let you know the abundant love that I have for you (2 Cor. 1:15—2:4).

Further, it is clear that the authority which the letter claims is inseparable from that authority which Paul claims as an apostle, and often as an apostle to that particular church to which he writes:

> For though absent in body I am present in spirit, and as if present, I have already pronounced judgment in the name of the Lord Jesus on the man who has done such a thing (1 Cor. 5:3–4a).

(In the case of 1 Corinthians, Paul often seems to be answering questions directed to him by the Corinthian church, and in answering he draws on his personal apostolic authority. The power of the letter depends on the assumption that Paul is one whose answers carry authority and that he can write assuming that same authority his answers would have were he in Corinth delivering the answers personally.)

All this is to propose that the very form of the epistle suggests a kind of authority of witness. What is said is important and valuable, but its importance and value depend in large measure upon *who* says it. Paul claims authority in his letters because he claims personal authority in those churches to which he writes, and the reason his letters should demand attention and obedience is that he himself as apostle thinks it right to demand attention and obedience from his churches.

Moreover, while Paul does not dwell on his personal experience or history, there are places where the authority of the letters depends quite concretely on the congruity of what Paul says with Paul's own history and experience.[14]

One crucial instance of such testimony is found in the Epistle to the Galatians. Hans Dieter Betz argues persuasively that Galatians is in large measure to be understood according to the structure and norm of the Hellenistic or Roman "apologetic letter." The way in which Betz describes the apologetic letter fits remarkably well with my description of that situation which calls forth the testimony of the witness and with my discussion of the letter as a substitute for the presence of the apostle himself:

> The function of the letter as letter implies also that the sender and the addressee are unable to have an oral conversation. The letter is a necessary substitute for such an oral exchange. By necessity, therefore, the letter is reductive. The letter represents its author, yet cannot act and react as its author might in person. Thus, the sender expresses himself *in absentia* and without the full range of communicative devices which an oral conversation can provide. The letter represents its author, without being able to act and react as an author.
>
> The apologetic letter, such as Galatians, presupposes the real or fictitious situation of the court of law, with jury, accuser and defendant. In the case of Galatians, the addressees are identical with the jury, with Paul being the defendant, and his opponents the accusers. This situation makes Paul's Galatian letter a self-apology, delivered not in person but in a written form.[15]

The place where Paul argues most like a "witness" in Galatians is in what Betz analyzes as the *narratio*—Gal. 1:12—2:14. The purpose of this narration, according to Betz, is to recite those facts which have a bearing on the defense which the letter makes, "in order to make the denial (of the charges brought against Paul) plausible." The purpose, of course, is not only instruction but also persuasion.[16]

In Galatians the *narratio* is presented to support Paul's fundamental claim against his opponents: "For I would have you know, brethren, that the gospel which was preached by me is not man's gospel" (Gal. 1:11). Paul's opponents apparently think his apostolic authority should be subject to the approval of the other apostles. But Paul then presents those facts from his history which support his claim of independence: the story of a call to apostleship which came not from any of the existing apostles but directly from Jesus Christ; the fact that even after his call he did not think it necessary to confer with the apostolic leadership in Jerusalem for three years. Then the argument gets a little more complicated. In 2:1–10, Paul argues that although he need not recognize the authority of the apostles at Jerusalem, in fact they did know of the gospel he preached and they did approve of his preaching that gospel as he did.

In Gal. 2:11–16, a somewhat different kind of defense begins to emerge. Paul is no longer primarily supporting the initial claim that his apostleship does not come from God; he begins to support a claim which is central to the material dispute between him and his opponents in Galatians. The material dispute rests on the question whether Gentile converts to Christianity should be subject to (certain portions) of the Jewish Law. Paul now argues that not only he but also Peter, one of the most honored of the earlier apostles, has held that Gentile converts need not submit to the Jewish Law. In fact both Paul and Peter stood apart from the requirements of the Law in their willingness to eat with Gentiles, until some more strictly Jewish Christians came to Antioch to visit Peter and Paul. At that point Paul continued to eat with Gentiles as he had before while Peter, cowardly, refused to live by his own convictions and withdrew from table fellowship with Gentile Christians.

Both in defending his own authority and in defending a gospel for the Gentiles which does not require obedience to the Jewish Law, Paul insists here on the congruity between his life and his claims. His first claim is that his authority does not depend on the approval of the older Jewish-Christian apostles who might or might not like his version of the gospel to the Gentiles. His history is congruent with that claim because he was not called to apostleship by them nor was his apostleship subject to their instruction or approval (though, incidentally, when he did mention to them what he was doing they did approve). Paul's second claim is that the gospel preached to the Gentiles ought not to demand of them obedience to the Jewish Law. His behavior has been congruent with that claim in that he willingly joins Gentiles at table fellowship. On the other hand Peter—presumably one of the authorities Paul's opponents would cite—actually agrees with Paul on this issue, but his behavior is *not* congruent with his belief, because when he feels pressure Peter yields and refuses to live according to his own convictions.

The *narratio*, as Betz would argue, is a clever attempt at persuasion. It presents the facts as facts but presents them in such a way as to make a point. Paul downplays the fact that he did test his gospel with the Jerusalem authorities at least once; he sneaks in the reminder that Peter—one of those authorities—does not have the courage of his convictions though his convictions actually coincide with Paul's.

Yet with all the rhetorical cleverness there does emerge a testimony in the richer sense of the word: "Here is what I claim," says Paul. "Here is what I am. Test what I claim by what I am; I am confident that you will see that the two coincide."

Again in 2 Corinthians we find Paul defending himself against opponents who belittle both him and his apostleship, and again we find him appealing to the congruity between what he preaches and the life he lives. Here opponents apparently have claimed that they are better apostles than Paul because of the power of their rhetoric and of the miracles which they have been able to perform among the Corinthians.[17] Paul responds in 2 Cor. 11:21—12:10.

The passage is highly rhetorical. Paul takes on the role of the "fool," though obviously he thinks he is far less foolish than his opponents and while refusing to boast he boasts, not so much of himself, as of the weakness which shows forth the power and grace of God (11:30, 12:1-10).

It is clear, however, that what Paul here argues for is precisely his integrity as a witness, the congruity between what he proclaims and what he is. In part this congruity is argued on the evidence of how much Paul has willingly suffered for the gospel he proclaims: "Are they servants of Christ? I am a better one . . . with far great labors, far more imprisonments . . . " (11:23). Here the close connection between the Greek word for "witness" (*martus*) and our word "martyr" becomes very clear. Part of Paul's claim to be a true witness rests on the evidence of his willingness to suffer for what he proclaims. If he has borne all this for what he preaches, then, he suggests, there can be no denying the depth of his conviction and, by implication, the validity of his apostleship.

There is another kind of congruity suggested by this passage—not only the congruity between Paul's convictions and his actions, but also a congruity between the shape of the gospel which he preaches and the shape of the life which he lives. Key phrases from Paul's testimony—weakness and foolishness—call to mind Paul's proclamation of the gospel in his earlier letter to the church at Corinth, summed up in 1 Cor. 1:22-25:

> For Jews demand signs and Greeks seek wisdom, but we preach Christ crucified, a stumbling block to Jews and folly to Gentiles, but to those who

are called, both Jews and Greeks, Christ the power of God and the wisdom of God. For the foolishness of God is wiser than men, and the weakness of God is stronger than men.

Implicitly but pervasively Paul argues in 2 Corinthians that his apostleship shows forth the claims of the gospel. In him, as in the cross of Christ, God's wisdom is made manifest in foolishness and God's power is made manifest in weakness.[18] Paul is the true and faithful witness, not because he is exceedingly wise and a powerful worker of miracles; those presumably are claims his opponents would make for themselves. Paul is the true and faithful witness because his life lives out the gospel which he proclaims, and the final ground of his boasting is the ground of his faith—the power of God made manifest primarily in Jesus Christ, but secondarily made manifest in Christ's servant Paul:

> For the sake of Christ, then, I am content with weaknesses, insults, hardships, persecutions, and calamities; for when I am weak, then I am strong (2 Cor. 12:10).[19]

Finally, it is evident throughout this passage in 2 Corinthians that Paul is precisely in the position of one arguing a case before a putative court of law. Here the case he argues is the validity of his own apostleship, and those who try him are the Corinthians themselves. The opponents stand throughout the epistle in the role of Paul's accusers. Paul defends both the truth of the gospel he proclaims and his truthfulness as a trustworthy witness. All this comes to a climax in 2 Corinthians 13, where Paul also calls Christ as witness on his behalf:

> This is the third time I am coming to you. Any charge must be sustained by the evidence of two or three witnesses. I warned those who sinned before and all the others, and I warn them now while absent, as I did when present on my second visit, that if I come again I will not spare them—since you desire proof that Christ is speaking in me. He is not weak in dealing with you, but is powerful in you. For he was crucified in weakness, but lives by the power of God. For we are weak in him, but in dealing with you we shall live with him by the power of God (2 Cor. 13:1–4).

Paul here nicely also reverses the roles of the "courtroom" where he pleads. No longer the defendant, he has now become judge, with the power of Christ, and it is no longer he who is on trial, it is the Corinthians. They had best attend to their faith lest he judge them severely.

In all these ways, these passages from 2 Corinthians point to the particular authority of witness. The apostle defends what he says and defends it by an appeal to the life he lives. The test of what he says is to be found in part in his life: if the readers, the jury, can see the integrity of the man, the correlation between what he says and what he is, then they will judge him to be vindicated.

THE AUTHORITY OF WITNESS TODAY

At the beginning of this chapter, I suggested that the analogy of a trial is particularly helpful in understanding the nature of the literature of witness. The imagery of the courtroom can also provide some initial insights into the authority which the literature of witness can have in the church today.

THE READER AS JURY

I suggested that one role of the literature of witness is to present the reader with two questions: (1) Is the testimony true? (2) Is the witness trustworthy?

The first question which such literature raises for the contemporary reader is the same question it raised for its original audience: Is this testimony convincing? Do I find this evidence persuasive?

Part of Jeremiah's testimony pointed to what God would do in history. Jeremiah's people, according to his claim, would be delivered to Nebuchadnezzar, the King of Babylon. One reason Jeremiah was preserved among the canonical prophets was that history bore out the accuracy of his predictions. We are interested in this man and his confessions in part because we know on other grounds that his testimony often turned out to be true.

Paul also wishes to point to the evidence of history, particularly to God's activity in Jesus Christ. In pointing to Jesus Christ, Paul thinks that he is pointing to evidence which the reader (the "jury") ought to be able to affirm as valid and convincing. If the evidence is not convincing, the fault lies not with the evidence but with the jury: "O foolish Galatians! Who has bewitched you, before whose eyes Jesus Christ was publicly portrayed as crucified?" (Gal. 3:1).

Yet in each case, the reader is called not only to believe in the truth of the testimony, but also to affirm the trustworthiness of the one who bears that testimony. The validity of Jeremiah's prophecy is further confirmed because the pain and judgment and modest hope which he prophesies are mirrored in the pain and judgment and modest hope which he shows forth in his experience. Like the most persuasive biographies or autobiographies, the literature of witness works most effectively when the shape of the life we discern fits the shape of the convictions which the subject declares. The test of such authority is whether the prophet, the witness, is as good as his or her word.

In making his claim for the significance of what God has done in Jesus Christ, Paul draws on a great variety of warrants. One such warrant is the warrant of his own experience. It is not only the report of Christ crucified and risen, it is Paul's experience of Christ which claims authority in Paul's testimony.

> For I through the law died to the law, that I might live to God. I have been crucified with Christ; it is no longer I who live, but Christ who lives in me; and the life I now live in the flesh I live by faith in the Son of God, who loved me and gave himself for me. I do not nullify the grace of God; for if justification were through the law, then Christ died to no purpose (Gal. 2:19–21).

One reason that Paul's writings have been so influential in the history of the church is that his epistles require us to see something of the personal effect of the gospel. Here, uniquely in the New Testament, we have the unmediated testimony of one believer to his own experience. The specific shape of that experience also has power because it can be seen to conform, however imperfectly, to the shape of the gospel Paul proclaims. Paul can speak against the power of the Law though he himself had gloried in the Law. He can speak of the redemptive suffering of the cross, himself having suffered. He can proclaim the weakness of God which is stronger than humankind, himself being tempted to strength and suffering from weakness. Paul does prove to be as good as his word, and the authority of his testimony derives in large measure from the fact that the discerning reader can see the congruity between what Paul claims to believe and the life he actually lives. The jury, reading Paul, is apt to decide that the witness is honest, and this helps toward the decision that the testimony is also true.

It is of the nature of testimony that it does not have the same indubitable nature that we tend to attribute to the evidences of science. The case comes before the jury, and the jury is bound to decide. In different ways, the Book of Jeremiah and the Epistles of Paul make their cases. But in different ways each derives its authority from the claim that Jeremiah or Paul was as good as his word. The authority of this literature in the church today derives in large measure from the fact that readers continue to affirm the trustworthiness of the witness and therefore to decide for the truth of the testimony which the witness brings.

TESTING THE TESTIMONY

The decision which the "jury" must make in reading the literature of witness is not only a decision about the one who testifies, it is a decision about the reader's life as well. Is this testimony sufficiently compelling that I can test it in my own experience? Will these words prove good for me, as well?

Paul clearly not only maintains the congruity between his own experience and the gospel he proclaims but he also invites the readers to enter into that experience and in so doing to discover for themselves the truth of the gospel. In Galatians, Paul constantly recalls the Galatian Christians to the truth of the gospel, not only by appeal to his experience in faith but also by a reminder of their own experience and by an urgent exhortation not to go back on the grace they have already obtained:

> Let me ask you only this: Did you receive the Spirit by works of the law, or by hearing with faith? Are you so foolish? Having begun with the Spirit, are you now ending with the flesh? Did you experience so many things in vain?— if it really is in vain (Gal. 3:2–4).

Paul makes explicit the relationship between his gospel, his experience, and the experience and commitment of his churches:

> I do not write this to make you ashamed, but to admonish you as my beloved children. For though you have countless guides in Christ, you do not have many fathers. For I became your father in Christ Jesus through the gospel. I urge you, then, be imitators of me (1 Cor. 4:14–16; cf. 1 Cor. 10:33— 11:1).

In the case of Jeremiah, the relationship between the experience of the prophet and the experience of the reader is less explicit. For instance, Jeremiah speaks an oracle to his disciple Baruch, one which strongly suggests that Baruch will know in his own experience that difficult relationship with the Lord which Jeremiah has known in his experience:

> "Thus says the LORD, the God of Israel, to you, O Baruch: You said, 'Woe is me! for the LORD has added sorrow to my pain; I am weary with my groaning, and I find no rest.' Thus shall you say to him, Thus says the LORD: Behold, what I have built I am breaking down, and what I have planted I am plucking up—that is, the whole land. And do you seek great things for yourself? Seek them not; for, behold, I am bringing evil upon all flesh, says the LORD; but I will give you your life as a prize of war in all places to which you may go" (Jer. 45:2–5).

Baruch surely foreshadows the experience of Judaism and of Christianity and the experience of many individual believers. Suffering and defeat in human history and in one's own life may not be a denial of the godhood of God. They may, on the contrary, reflect the terms by which God chooses to deal with humankind. Thus the experience of later generations of readers confirm the experience both of Jeremiah and of his disciple.

All this is to suggest that one way in which the literature of testimony has authority is that it not only shows forth the congruity between the life and the words of the witness, it causes the reader to test out that congruity in his or her own experience. In this way, to return to our analogy, the reader is no longer jury, but defendant, and the question is not only, "What shall we do with the witness?" but also, "What shall we do with ourselves?" The test of the testimony is not only in the life of the witness but in the lives of those who hear.

TESTIMONY AND TRUST

I have suggested that the authority of words calls for faithful hearing. The authority of deeds calls for discernment of God's activity in history. The authority of story calls for the identification of the reader with the figures in the story. The authority of wisdom relies on the common sense of the community which learns and shares wisdom.

One way to understand the authority of witness is to suggest that it calls primarily for trust. The reader or listener is asked first to trust the testimony which the literature of witness brings—to trust the claim that God brings judgment and quiet hope, or the claim that God's grace and power are made known in weakness.

Two warrants, however, are used to make the case for trust more compelling. As readers or listeners we are asked to trust the testimony because we trust the testifier. The literature shows the congruity between the words spoken and the one who speaks and encourages us to acknowledge that the speaker is trustworthy. Thereby our trust in the testimony is engaged. And we are asked to test the testimony by trusting our own lives to the claims which the witness makes, by proving in our own experience the validity of the witness' experience.

Here trust becomes a kind of entrustment, and the biblical literature of witness would claim that this trusting of our lives is not only finally a matter of trusting the witness and his testimony, it is also finally a way of entrusting our lives to God, to whom the witness testifies:

> For what we preach is not ourselves, but Jesus Christ as Lord, with ourselves as your servants for Jesus' sake. For it is the God who said, "Let light shine out of darkness," who has shown in our hearts to give the light of the knowledge of the glory of God in the face of Christ (2 Cor. 4:5–6).

NOTES

1. Strictly speaking, "wisdom" literature is not all of one genre either, but rather presents a particular perspective on God's relationship to the world in diverse literary forms. Cf. the discussion in Gerhard von Rad, *Wisdom in Israel,* (Nashville: Abingdon Press, 1972), 24–52.

2. Much of this analysis is similar to and informed by Paul Ricoeur's essay, "The Hermeneutics of Testimony" in *Essays on Biblical Interpretation,* edited by Lewis S. Mudge (Philadelphia: Fortress Press, 1980), 119–154. Ricoeur here, however, is not dealing with a particular type of biblical literature but with the nature of a broad range of religious language and the relationship of the question of testimony to certain larger hermeneutical questions.

3. The prophetic call narratives are somewhat an exception here, though these are fairly stylized and formal. Cf. Norman Habel, "The Form and Significance of the Call Narratives," *ZAW* 77/3 (1965), 297–323.

4. This hedges on the difficult question of why some parts of the Acts of the Apostles are written in the first person plural, but even if these represent an eyewitness testimony of the narrator, it is striking how little he as an individual can be discerned within the story which he tells.

5. G. von Rad includes Jer. 11:18–23, 12:1–6, 15:10–12, 15–21, 17:12–18, 18:18–23, 20:7–18. See Gerhard von Rad, *Old Testament Theology,* Vol. II, Eng. trans. D. M. G. Stalker (New York: Harper & Row; Edinburgh: Oliver & Boyd, 1965), 201–6.

6. Cf. von Rad, *Old Testament Theology,* 201.

7. Cf. von Rad, *Old Testament Theology,* 204.

8. John Bright, *Jeremiah* Anchor Bible (Garden City, N.Y.: Doubleday & Co., 1965), xix–xxi.

9. Von Rad, *Old Testament Theology,* II:208.

10. Von Rad, *Old Testament Theology,* II: 203.

11. Von Rad, *Old Testament Theology,* II:204.

12. As cited in F. Brown, S. Driver, and C. A. Briggs, *Hebrew and English Lexicon of the Old Testament* (Oxford: Clarendon Press, 1962), 103.

13. Robert Funk, "The Apostolic Parousia: Form and Significance" in W. R. Farmer, C. F. D. Moule and R. R. Niebuhr, eds., *Christian History and Interpretation* (New York and Cambridge: Cambridge University Press, 1967), 249–268. Cf. John L. White, *The Body of the Greek Letter,* SBLDS 2 (Missoula, Mont.: Scholars Press, 1972), 44.

14. On Paul's "reticence" cf. J. C. Beker, *Paul the Apostle: The Triumph of God in Life and Thought* (Philadelphia: Fortress Press, 1980), 3.

15. Hans Dieter Betz, *Galatians: A Commentary on Paul's Letter to the Churches at Galatia,* Hermeneia—A Historical-Critical Commentary on the Bible (Philadelphia: Fortress Press, 1979), 24. Betz goes on to argue that the apologetic letter is insufficient for the claims Paul wants to make and that Galatians is therefore also a "magical" letter, with a curse for Paul's opponents and a blessing for those who are faithful to his gospel.

16. Betz, *Galatians,* 59.

17. For a very influential discussion of Paul's opponents, cf. Dieter Georgi, *Die Gegner des Paulus in 2 Korintherbrief: Studien zur religiösen Propaganda in der Spätantiken.* WMANT 11 (Neukirchen-Vluyn: Neukirchener, 1964). Summarized by Georgi in

his article "Corinthians, Second" in *The Interpreters Dictionary of the Bible-Supplementary Volume* (Nashville: Abingdon Press, 1976), 184–85.

18. Similarly in 1 Corinthians 2, Paul's preaching takes on the shape of the gospel; it too is weak and foolish but shows forth the power of God (1 Cor. 2:1–5).

19. For a persuasive discussion of the way in which Paul's apostleship takes on the shape of the gospel he preaches, cf. John Howard Schütz, *Paul and the Anatomy of Apostolic Authority,* SNTSMS (New York and Cambridge: Cambridge University Press, 1975), 282, et passim.

6 / Canon and Community

The argument of this book thus far could easily lead to two mistaken assumptions. First, one might assume that the question of biblical authority is a question primarily for the individual reader of Scripture. How does the Bible speak to me and my condition? Second, one might assume that the question of biblical authority is exclusively a question about the diverse specific types of biblical literature, taken in isolation from one another. How are the parables authoritative for a Christian today? Or, how does wisdom literature inform contemporary ethical reflection?

However, a more accurate view of scriptural authority would question both these assumptions. The assumption that scriptural authority is an individual matter is challenged by the reminder that, from the beginning, *communities* of believers passed on authoritative traditions, shaped those traditions into books, decided which books should count as Scripture, and provided the context for interpreting the Scripture generation after generation.

The assumption that the specific types of biblical literature can be studied and interpreted in isolation from one another is challenged by the reminder that the communities which passed on, shaped, and acknowledged those traditions acknowledged that the rich diversity of literature served together as Scripture.

That diverse collection of books which the church now acknowledges to have ongoing authority is called "the canon." Strictly speaking, a canon is a normative collection of writings, providing the authoritative source for Christian reflection and practice and the measure by which other Christian literature can be tested.[1] The precise list of books to be included in the canon was not decided at any council of the church until the Roman Catholic Church officially adopted a canon at the Council of Trent in 1546.[2] By the end of the fourth century, however, the books to be included in the New Testament canon for the Eastern church had been largely settled, and by the early fifth century the issue had been largely settled for the Latin church.[3]

Long before the virtual settling of the canonical list, the issue of what would count as authoritative Scripture was a central concern of the emerging Christian church. The ways in which the church decided what traditions and books would be authoritative may be helpful to our contemporary reflection on the authoritative status of the canon.

For the earliest Christians, *Scripture* was Hebrew Scripture (sometimes in Greek translation, as in the Septuagint). It is not at all clear that the synagogue had yet established the precise extent of its "canonical" Scripture, but the earliest Christians assumed that the Scripture of Judaism was their Scripture, too.

Among Jewish Christians it is not surprising that the authority of the Hebrew Bible was assumed. What is more remarkable is that the earliest evidence we have of the nature of Gentile Christianity indicates that Gentile Christians also accepted the Hebrew Bible as authoritative for them. Therefore the earliest Christian writings take it for granted that to understand Jesus Christ and God's activity in him, one must accept the authority of the Hebrew Bible.[4]

As early as our earliest source, the apostle Paul, we can see Christians appealing to another authority than that of Jewish Scripture—the authority of certain traditions about Jesus. In 1 Cor. 11:23–25, Paul passes on the tradition of Jesus' words at the supper on the night he was betrayed. In 1 Cor. 15:3–7, Paul passes on a somewhat modified tradition concerning Jesus' crucifixion, burial, and resurrection appearances. (In this latter case Paul appeals *both* to the tradition about Jesus and to Jewish Scripture; Christ's death and resurrection happened "according to the scripture.") In 1 Cor. 7:10, Paul cites a saying attributed to Jesus to adjudicate a question about divorce: "To the married I give charge, not I but the Lord, that the wife should not separate from her husband . . . and that the husband should not divorce his wife."[5]

By the end of the first century, traditions about Jesus were edited and interpreted in gospels. Furthermore, now Paul himself, along with other apostles, was seen as an authoritative resource for Christian faith. Traditions about Paul and the other apostles were collected and edited in the Acts of the Apostles. Sometime in the second century, collections of letters attributed to Paul were circulated. Some were actually written by Paul; some were written by other Christians in his name, a tribute to his particular authority. During these same years, other Christian writings which did not become part of the New Testament canon were written and read in various Christian communities. At the same time oral traditions about Jesus, Paul, and other apostles continued to circulate. The church was aware of being under the continuing and direct influence of the Holy Spirit, and there was no apparent need to determine which books and which traditions were particularly authoritative.

Then a challenge from a second century theologian required Christians to think more seriously about what written material should and should not count as a source and resource for their faith. Marcion, who emerged as an influential thinker about A.D. 140, had read Paul and Paul's claims about the insufficiency of the Jewish Law. Marcion took Paul's criticism of the Law much farther than Paul ever did. He decided that the difference between the Law and the gospel of Jesus Christ proves that there is not one God but two, the God of the Old Testament and the God of Christians. The Old Testament God had to be abandoned. Along with the Old Testament God, Marcion abandoned the Old Testament. Along with the Old Testament, Marcion banned those portions of early Christian literature which seemed to rely unduly on the Old Testament as a source for their own reflection. What remained was a "canon" considerably smaller than the later canon of the church. Marcion included ten epistles attributed to Paul (not 1 and 2 Timothy or Titus) and one gospel, which was a condensed and purified version of the Gospel of Luke.[6]

In response to the challenge of Marcion and other second century theologians, various Christian leaders stressed the continued significance of the Old Testament for Christian faith and practice. Irenaeus, writing toward the end of the second century, further insisted that Christians recognize not one but four gospels.[7] The four gospels were not discovered only at that late date, of course. Apparently they were read and used in various churches and had already become an important source for Christian piety. It was Marcion and other threatening theologians who helped induce leaders such as Irenaeus to acknowledge that the four gospels already used among various churches were authoritative for the church. It is less clear what epistles Christians toward the end of the second century regarded as being authoritative.

The next challenge to the extent of Christian authoritative literature came from a group called the Montanists. This group emerged after the first half of the second century. They believed in the imminent end of the world and the second coming of Christ. They appealed especially to apocalyptic prophecies, that is, to prophecies which stressed the signs of the end of time.

Consequently, Christians who were disturbed by the Montanists (like Gaius of Rome, ca. A.D. 200) were unhappy with apocalyptic literature, including the Book of Revelation, and wanted to insist that such literature should not be normative for the church.[8] Indeed, the Book of Revelation remained the writing whose place in the canon was most disputed for many centuries to come.

Sometime not long after the Montanists, some Christian in Rome compiled a list of those books which could have authority for Scripture. The list is available to us only as a fragment. We do not know who wrote it, and we do not know who paid attention to it, but it does indicate that Christians were puzzling about what literature should have scriptural authority and were suggesting reasons for including this book or that in an authoritative collection. This list, called the Muratorian Canon, apparently assumes our four canonical gospels. It includes Paul's letters. It implies that Christian writings are now as authoritative for Christian people as are the books of the Old Testament.[9]

Certain features of the works on the list are cited to prove that they should be included in Christian Scripture. There is discussion of which writings are apostolic, but the point is not that the authors had to be apostles but that they had to belong to the apostolic time.[10] Paul's letters appear to pose a problem because they are directed to individual churches, while authoritative Scripture should apply to the whole church. However, the fact that Paul wrote seven letters (according to this list) indicates that Paul had the universal church in mind, as did John in writing the seven letters to the churches in Asia Minor, according to Revelation.[11] Finally, the Muratorian Canon discusses only those books which are actually used in the reading and worship of the church. It is the fact that the churches use these books which makes them candidates for authoritative status.

I have provided only a brief sketch of the earliest movements toward the establishment of a canon. The debate about specific books, especially Hebrews and Revelation, continued for some time, and the extent of the canon was not fixed for practical purposes until the fourth or fifth century.

However, even this brief historical sketch suggests something of the continuing significance of the canon for Christian reflection.

First, the implicit decision of the early church to take the Old Testament as authoritative Scripture was made explicit in the theological discussions following Marcion. The Christian canon included *both* the Old and the New Testaments.

Second, the "decisions" concerning what books should be included in the New Testament canon included two different kinds of impulse. There was the initial positive impulse which discerned the authoritative nature of a tradition or writing and sought to preserve that tradition or writing for future generations. Thus some of the sayings of Jesus and stories about him were collected and shaped in gospels. The Pauline letters were gathered in collections.

There was a second, negative, impulse. Christians sought to define the *limits* of what could count as an acceptable resource for faith in the threat of opposition which was perceived as heretical. In the face of Marcion, certain Christian leaders insisted on a more inclusive canon, one which had four gospels, epistles other than Paul's, and the Old Testament. In the face of the Montanists, certain Christians demanded a canon which excluded various apocalyptic writings; sometimes Revelation was among those excluded. One might say that the first movement, which affirms authoritative tradition, inevitably leads to the second, which sets the appropriate limits of that tradition.

Third, the criteria for deciding what counted as canonical Scripture also help suggest the ongoing function of canonical Scripture.

1. The only candidates for canonical status were writings which were actually used in the churches. Certain books already *had* authority in the practice of believing communities: they were used for preaching, worship, and religious and moral guidance. Later the church acknowledged that some of these books *should* have authority for the whole church, should be used generally in preaching, worship, and religious and moral guidance. That is to say, initially certain books had practical authority within the believing communities. Later the church acknowledged that many of these should have official authority as well, should be binding on the faith and practice of all Christians.[12]

2. The canon did set the outer limits of acceptable Christian belief and practice, but those limits bounded a considerable degree of ongoing and acceptable diversity. Indeed it was Marcion, whom the later church repudiated, who wanted to limit radically the range of diversity within Scripture.

3. The question of what books could count as authoritative was not directly the question of apostolic authorship. The question was not whether those who had written the gospels, for instance, had known Jesus. The question was whether they lived in the apostolic age, the period of the original witness.

4. Related to this is the claim which the Muratorian Canon makes regarding the universality of Paul's epistles. One mark of a canonical writing is that it be a writing which stands the test of time and of broad application. A book whose initial insights can be applied to the church in new situations and diverse places has a claim to canonical status.[13]

By this time a close connection between the community of faith and the canon becomes apparent. Historically it was the communities of faith—Israel, the synagogue, the church—which determined what books were authoritative for faith and practice. So, too, at the present time it is within the context of communities of faith that the ongoing discussion continues: How do we read, interpret, preach on the books which are included within the canon? How do we acknowledge the diversity of the canon and find ways of adjudicating its different alternatives for faith and practice? Is the canon still open to revision?

There is also the other side. Historically, various traditions and writings had proved themselves to be authoritative in the worship and practice of various communities before decisions were made to count them as "canonical." It is true that the church shaped the canon; but the writings which became canonical had already helped to shape the church.[14]

At the present time the church provides the context for interpretation and adjudication of questions of canonical authority. But the canon also shapes and influences the church. The canon provides Scripture for the church, provides the authoritative literature which helps Christian people and Christian churches judge the shape of their belief and practice. The very fact of the canon's diversity makes possible the diversity of Christian faith and practice. The fact that there *is* a canon provides a context within which Christians can argue with each other on the basis of appeal to an agreed authority. The appropriate ways of interpreting that authoritative canon are complex, but the fact that there is a body of literature to which Christians can appeal makes a sense of ongoing, ecumenical, argumentative community possible.

We can draw a rough analogy between the function of the canon with the believing community and the function of the Constitution for the United States. Just as citizens of the United States acknowledge the particular authority of the Constitution for their life and practice, so members of the Christian church, as members of the Christian church, acknowledge the particular authority of the canon for their life and practice. The canon—like the Constitution—is interpreted differently by different "citizens." The canon—like the Constitution—might conceivably be amended from time to time on the basis of new information, new needs, new insights. In the meantime, the canon, like the Constitution, has an authoritative function for the church. To be in the church is to acknowledge the significance of the canon.[15]

THE CANON AS A RESOURCE FOR THE COMMUNITY

The two fundamental issues raised by the foregoing sketch of the history of canon and community are these: (1) How does the canon provide a fundamental resource for the church's life and practice? (2) How does the community, the church, provide the context for the interpretation of the canon? This section addresses the first of those questions.

In recent years, especially in the work of Brevard Childs and James

Sanders, there has emerged a new stress on the canon as the proper context of biblical interpretation in the church.[16]

The stress on the canonical context of biblical interpretation suggests two claims. First, the *whole* canon provides the context for scriptural interpretation in the church. Second, Scripture *in its canonical form* provides the resource for faith and practice in the church. We shall examine each of these claims in turn.

A FIRST CLAIM

The suggestion that the church should use the whole canon in biblical interpretation derives from the assumption that the church's decision (however informal) on the limits of canon suggests not just what books are *possible* resources for Christian reflection; the church's decision regarding the canon dictates what books are fundamental resources for Christian reflection.[17] Preaching, worship, practice, theological reflection which base themselves exclusively on one portion of the canon (the New Testament to the exclusion of the Old; Paul to the exclusion of Matthew) are unfaithful to the church's understanding of the whole canon as authoritative Scripture. Both Old and New Testament are central to the church's faith and life. Galatians *and* the Pastorals; Matthew *and* John; Deuteronomy *and* Amos are essential resources for the church's reflection.

The place where we can most clearly agree in affirming the significance of the whole canon for the church is in the relationship of the Old to the New Testament. Here those who affirm a canonical interpretation of the Bible lay claim to a fundamental insight which is congruent with the history of Scripture in the church. The earliest practice of Gentile Christian churches and the response of the "catholic" church to Marcion indicate the church's conviction that the Old Testament provides an essential guide to Christian life and faith. It represents a fundamental presupposition for understanding what God has done in Christ. For example, Gerhard von Rad says, "Our knowledge of Christ is incomplete without the witness of the Old Testament. Christ is given to us only through the double witness of those who wait and those who remember."[18]

Furthermore, the early church's use of the Hebrew Bible as a resource for *Christian* reflection indicates that for the church, the "Old Testament" will always be understood in its relationship to the New. For the Christian it is the Old Testament which points to Christ, and it is to Christ that the Old Testament points.

It is not possible, however, for contemporary Christians to understand the Old Testament's "pointing" to Christ in precisely the ways that New

Testament writers understood it.[19] Study of Old Testament books in their historical context has indicated that prophetic passages which Christians thought pointed directly to Christ often point to some incident closer to the time of the prophet, or they point in general terms to an unspecified future. Arguments that specific features of the Old Testament, like the name of Melchizedek in Gen. 14:17–20, point directly to features of the New Testament story, like the priesthood of Jesus (Hebrews 7), seem to us clever but unconvincing.

If, however, we read the Bible as a whole canon, remembering the New Testament when we read the Old and the Old Testament when we read the New, it is impossible not to be aware of overtones, reminiscences, foreshadowings. The Christian interpreter cannot read the story of the binding of Isaac in Genesis 22 without recalling God's giving of *his* only son, proclaimed in John 3:16. The Christian cannot hear the familiar verse of Isaiah without hearing in those verses a hint of that redemption Christians acknowledge in Jesus Christ (however unintended by the prophet that hint might be):

> But he was wounded for our transgressions,
>   he was bruised for our iniquities;
> upon him was the chastisement that made us whole,
>   and with his stripes we are healed. (Isa. 53:5)

Considerable recent literature has been devoted to the attempt to discover systematic ways to link the Old and the New Testament. Some writers stress the relationship of both Testaments as records of the mighty acts of God.[20] Some stress motifs of prophecy and fulfillment, or of foreshadowing and recalling.[21]

Our study of the diversity of biblical literature suggests that *no* single overarching scheme of the relationship of the two Testaments will be adequate as a guide to canonical interpretation. A whole range of questions becomes appropriate to the task: Where does the New Testament quote the Old? What is assumed in these quotations? Where are Old Testament stories retold or reshaped or alluded to in the New Testament? Where do Old Testament literary forms (miracle stories, prophetic judgment sayings) influence the forms of New Testament literature? Where does the New Testament rely on types of argument or persuasion already employed in the Old Testament? How do various New Testament writers understand law, both Old Testament Torah and Christian "law"? What devices in the exegesis of other interpreters of the Old Testament who wrote before or during New Testament times help us to understand the interpretive devices of New Testament writers? Any attempt to find a single interpretive clue risks ignoring the rich variety of relationships between Old and New Testament literature. The work of interpretation within the canonical context will probably demand more modest, inductive exegetical endeavors.[22]

If we can unreservedly affirm the claim of canonical critics that Christian scriptural interpretation needs to pay close attention to both Old and New Testaments, it is harder to affirm unconditionally the claim that Christian interpretation and preaching needs to pay (equal?) attention to the whole range of biblical literature—Paul and James; Matthew and John; Deuteronomy and Job. While it *seems* that the whole canon should provide a resource for Christian reflection and proclamation, on further reflection problems emerge.

An example will indicate the problems which such canonical interpretation might involve.

Both Paul's writings and the Epistle of James pay considerable attention to the relationship of faith and works for the Christian:

> What then shall we say about Abraham, our forefather according to the flesh? For if Abraham was justified by works, he had something to boast about, but not before God. For what does the scripture say? "Abraham believed God, and it was reckoned to him as righteousness." Now to one who works, his wages are not reckoned as a gift but as his due. And to one who does not work but trusts him who justifies the ungodly, his faith is reckoned as righteousness. . . .
>
> The promise to Abraham and his descendants, that they should inherit the world, did not come through the law but through the righteousness of faith (Rom. 4:1–5, 13).

> Was not Abraham our father justified by works, when he offered his son Isaac upon the altar? You see that faith was active along with his works, and faith was completed by works, and the scripture was fulfilled which says, "Abraham believed God, and it was reckoned to him as righteousness" (James 2:21–23).

Perhaps it cannot be said that James and Paul directly contradict each other, since they do not understand exactly the same thing by the term "works." However it is clear that the Epistle of James (which was written after Paul) intends to correct Paul and to suggest that a Pauline understanding of faith is inadequate and even mistaken. One can appreciate James' hesitation about embracing Paul's insistence on justification by faith, but one cannot affirm that James and Romans provide equally adequate statements of the relationship of faith to works. One cannot hold them as equally central or valid statements even within the diversity of the canon. The one understanding largely excludes the other.

Nor is it sufficient to say that we can look to the portraits of Jesus in the Gospels as the norm for reading Scripture and test other scriptural passages by those portraits. For the four Gospels at some points present radically different understandings of Jesus' ministry, death, and resurrection.

For instance, as we have seen (cf. Chapter 3, pp. 52–59 above), it is clear that Mark and Luke have very different understandings of Jesus' crucifixion. For Mark it was a moment of the most extreme suffering and abandonment. Precisely that suffering and abandonment indicated to the centurion that the crucified one was God's son. For Luke the crucifixion was a moment of faithful martyrdom. Jesus speaks words of courageous resignation. The centurion is not convicted of faith but is convinced of the innocence of the victim.

In the Gospels, as in the Bible generally, quite divergent perspectives on faith and practice are present. It is not possible for careful readers of the texts to maintain that all these perspectives are equally valid. Some principle of selection or interpretation is necessary.

Recognizing that need, scriptural interpreters have suggested two rather different strategies for dealing with the diversity and even the conflicts among biblical motifs and claims.

Some scholars suggest that there are fundamental motifs or organizing principles which are central to Scripture. In the light of these motifs, other subsidiary ideas take their proper place.

For G. Ernest Wright and Reginald Fuller, the fundamental motif in Scripture is the motif of the God who acts.

> The Bible is a "historical" literature in which God is proclaimed as the chief actor in history who alone gives history its meaning. To study the Bible is such a way as to make abstractions of its spiritual or moral teachings, divorced from their real context of their setting in time is to turn the Bible into a book of aphorisms, full of nice sayings, which the devil himself could believe and never find himself particularly handicapped either by the knowledge of them or by their repetition.[23]

(That God does not act precisely as other historical agents act is part of what makes the interpretation of biblical history complicated, as Fuller and Wright acknowledge [cf. Chapter 3, above].)

For Walter Eichrodt, at least one fundamental organizing theme for Scripture is the motif of covenant, that contract between God and humankind which begins in the stories of the Old Testament and is fulfilled in Jesus Christ and the church as the community of the New Covenant.[24]

For Samuel Terrien, the fundamental motif uniting Scripture and providing its central insights is the motif of the (paradoxical) revelation of the hidden God.[25]

Each of these writers suggests that the way to deal with the diversity of Scripture is to discern a central, organizing principle and to stress those elements in Scripture which accord with that principle.

Implicit within the work of those who find organizing themes for Scripture is the claim that some portions of the canon have more validity and power as resources for Christian thought and life than other portions. What these writers suggest implicitly other interpreters make explicit. They refer to what is called "a canon within the canon." They ask the question: within the diversity of biblical literature, what are those books or motifs whose validity is fundamental for understanding the Christian faith? Then they judge the validity and truthfulness of other portions of Scripture on the basis of this "canon"—this normative text or theme—within the larger canon of Scripture.

The suggestion of a canon within a canon derives in part from the writings of Martin Luther. For Luther the central "canon within the canon" was the good news of Jesus Christ. It is the fact that a text presents Christ which makes that text normative for faith and action:

> All the genuine sacred books agree in this that all of them preach Christ and deal with Him. That is the true test by which to judge all books, when we see whether they deal with Christ or not, since all the Scriptures show us Christ, and St. Paul will know nothing but Christ. What does not teach Christ is not apostolic even though St. Peter or St. Paul taught it; again, what preaches Christ would be apostolic even though Judas, Annas, Pilate and Herod did it.[26]

Contemporary scholars, also stressing the centrality of Christ as a "canon within the canon," a norm within the Bible, have interpreted that norm in different ways.

Joachim Jeremias seeks a canon within the canon (or more accurately, a canon *behind* the canon) in what he can reconstruct of the teaching of the historical Jesus.

> For faith there is no authority but the Lord. The historical Jesus and his message are not one presupposition among many for the Kerygma, but the sole presupposition of the Kerygma. . . . Only the Son of Man and His Word can give authority to the message—no one else and nothing else.[27]

Ernst Käsemann, more in accord with Luther, claims that it is not the reconstruction of the message of Jesus which provides the norm for scriptural interpretation, but the good news of Jesus Christ as the one whose crucifixion reconciles ungodly humankind to God.

> The central message of the Bible is that God deals always, indeed exclusively, with the godless, because before him no man is pious and just.[28]

> The Bible, too, preserves after its own fashion the lowliness and the hiddenness of the crucified Jesus. God speaks through it, as through the earthly Jesus, out of darkness, and hides himself in it as in the earthly Jesus and his Cross. Only by building on this foundation shall we be able to hear God proclaiming the Gospel from within the Canon. Otherwise we are bound to lose the Gospel for the sake of the Canon.[29]

Everything we have said about the diversity of Scripture and the particular problems we noted above regarding the strongly different emphases of James and Romans, or of Mark and Luke, suggests that the search for a canon within the canon is a necessary part of the task of scriptural interpretation, a task which canonical interpretation needs to take into account.

Our sketch of the history of the development of Scripture and the canon suggests some guidelines for any Christian or any Christian community which seeks to affirm a canon within the canon.

1. Any appropriate canon within the canon will center in the good news of God's activity in Jesus Christ. For the church the fundamental encounter of God with humankind is the encounter in Jesus Christ. Scripture, as von Rad noted, includes the witness of those who wait and those who remember, but for Christians what is essential is that the witnesses await and remember Jesus Christ. The history of the formation of the canon suggests the same centrality of the good news of Jesus Christ. The Old Testament from the start was seen as a source of reflection on what God had done in Jesus Christ. Books were chosen for the New Testament canon on the assumption that they faithfully witnessed to him.

One can make a similar point in terms of an understanding of the church. For the church, the center of life is obedient faith to the God who reconciles humans to God in Jesus Christ. The center of the church's preaching is the good news of Jesus Christ. Scripture's fundamental importance is as a resource for living, believing, and preaching. Scripture's center must therefore be Christ. Any attempt to read Scripture predominantly as a resource for reconstructing the spiritual evolution of near-eastern and Hellenistic peoples, or primarily as a guide to general ethical conduct, or even as a list of various important acts of God, is incongruent with the church's insistence that the canon provides its scripture as a *Christian* community.

2. Any further decision on a canon within the canon, and some further decision is necessary,[30] will require theological and not simply historical reflection. Even if one could be more convinced than I am that Jeremias has discovered the essential shape of Jesus' teaching, the fact that such teaching preceded the early church's preaching, or the writing of Paul's epistles, or the writing of the gospels, does not in itself prove that Jesus' teaching should provide the norm for Christian scriptural interpretation. Nothing in the earliest strata of the Jesus tradition or the accuracy of a scholarly reconstruction of that tradition indicates that in itself such a tradition is a more valuable center for Christian faith than, say, John's insistence that Jesus was the incarnate Word, or Paul's representation of the crucified and risen Lord as one who frees people from the law by the gift of God's grace. Arguments can be held and reasons cited for holding one portrait of Christ to be more adequate than another as the basis for a canon within the canon. Evidence about chronology does not serve to settle that argument.

3. We have been at pains to insist that the Bible does not belong to individuals but to the church. More than that, the Bible is interpreted within denominational communions and in the light of confessional traditions. It is not possible to stand in *the* church without also standing in *a* church, and the shape of that church's theology will rightly affect one's understanding of a canon within the canon. Käsemann, as a committed Lutheran, sees his understanding of the center of the canon to be in line with Martin Luther's own concerns. Baptists, who sometimes think of themselves as reflecting the practice of the early church, love to appeal to Luke, where Jesus founds the church, and to Acts, where (Baptists believe) the apostles act like Baptists. Hans Küng, as a Roman Catholic, appeals to the catholicity of the canon, insisting that its very diversity provides its universality. For Küng, some documents which Käsemann judges to be inferior are of ongoing significance.[31] Part of the task of finding a canon within a canon is to find one's relationship to one's own specific community of faith.

4. Any adequate interpretation of a canon within the canon will require attention to the second "canon" in that phrase, as well as to the first. For the individual Christian, this suggests that he or she will constantly be open to the possibility that positions firmly held and stoutly defended will need revision in the light of other claims contained within the larger canon of Christian Scripture. Or it may be that some portion of Scripture which had

always seemed opaque will become suddenly transparent, illuminating, or helpful. Karl Barth pictures this process in the Christian interpretation of Scripture:

[As newcomers to faith] we shall find the further witness of Revelation which the Church promises us only in definite parts of the Canon indicated to us, but in others we shall not find it. . . . If this is really the case, if we think we have received a direct confirmation in respect of at any rate a smaller part of what is proposed (let us say in respect of certain psalms, or gospels, or epistles, or even specific passages in these books) this may incline us to judge favourably in respect of the rest of what is proposed. And this pre-judgment will at once acquire a practical significance if it is not just a matter of our opinion . . . if in hearing [these portions of scripture] we have really come to the obedience of faith. Placed in this obedience and *ipso facto* brought into agreement, even if only partial, with the witness of the Church, we shall definitely be ready to hear further this witness in regard to the Canon, and therefore not to cease but to continue searching the witness of the Word of God in those parts of the proposed Canon so far closed to us.[32]

For congregations, communions, and denominations, part of the task of interpreting the canon *within* the canon will be to enter into conversation with Christians who use and defend a different canon within the canon. One way to increase church unity is to enter into ongoing discussion with each other. What motifs, perspectives, or passages of Scripture are central to our community and its understanding? How do these relate to your community's scriptural allegiances? Where can we learn from each other? Where can we correct each other? Where must we acknowledge legitimate differences?[33] If the canon should never be closed because of the ongoing presence of the Holy Spirit, surely the canon within the canon can never be closed, either for individual Christians or for the communities of faith.

5. The various understandings of canon within the canon represent different understandings of the *function* of Scripture for the community. Those who want to stress questions of ethics or personal relationships tend to look to Jesus as an ethical teacher or as supremely human and humanizing.[34] Those who discern the fundamental human dilemma to be sinfulness stress the forgiveness and reconciliation which comes in Jesus Christ. Those who are predominantly concerned with oppressive social structures see in Jesus the message and the personification of personal and social liberation.

Any decision concerning our own canon within the canon will be aided if we can be self-conscious about the problems we are asking Scripture to address. (What we have seen of the variety of scriptural literature suggests that there is no one "right" problem to which Scripture attends.) Any discussion of canonical interpretation with other Christians or other denominations will be aided by the attempt to raise clearly the question of what purpose Scripture and scriptural interpretation are intended to serve.

6. Any decision regarding a canon within the canon will also reflect the historical and social circumstances of the person or community who makes that decision. Martin Luther's stress on the centrality of Paul's view of justification by faith resulted in part from the particular historical circumstances of the Roman Catholic Church in the 16th century. John Calvin's view of the law, which was more favorable than Luther's, perhaps resulted in part from his role as a leader of a Christian city in Geneva. Walter Rauschenbusch's strong stress on a particular reading of the teachings about the kingdom of God was conditioned in part by his service as a pastor in Hell's Kitchen in New York and his sense of the necessity for the gospel to address social change.

A right understanding of a canon within the canon will recognize the historical circumstances which help suggest a particular center for Scripture. Faithful Christians will acknowledge that new historical circumstances may force them to shift that center. Christians in conversation with one another will acknowledge that as individuals and communities we live in somewhat different histories and therefore we look for somewhat different centers in our Scripture.

This discussion of the role of a canon within the canon again recalls my analogy between the canon for the church and the Constitution for the United States.

While in principle all citizens of the United States acknowledge the authority of the whole Constitution, in fact different citizens, different groups or parties stress different elements of that Constitution. Some stress the first amendment's guarantees of liberties. Some stress the Preamble's clause on domestic tranquillity (law and order). Some even stress (and misinterpret) the right to bear arms. The ongoing debate about the appropriate function of government and the appropriate shape of citizenship includes the debate over which elements of the Constitution are to be interpreted as centrally important and which have lesser status.

Furthermore, in constitutional interpretation as in the church, the "canon within the canon" can shift with shifting historical circumstances. In recent years the fourteenth amendment became exceedingly important as a guide to adjudicating debates about civil rights. At the turn of the century, the clause regarding Congress' right to regulate interstate commerce provided a guideline for anti-trust legislation.

From time to time it is possible to amend the Constitution, as in principle it is possible to amend the canon,[35] but in the meantime citizens assume its validity, argue about its interpretation, disagree regarding what is central and what is peripheral, and change their minds about what is central on the basis of shifting historical circumstance.

What holds the nation together is the allegiance to the document itself and the willingness to debate its interpretation. One thing which holds the church together, beyond the grace of God and loyalty to Jesus Christ, is the acknowledgement of the particular role of canon and the willingness to debate its interpretation.

With those who recall us to the canon as a context of interpretation, we would maintain that the entire canon has a particular role as a source and resource for Christian life and practice. We would further acknowledge that each Christian and each Christian community will find some organizing principle or some "canon within the canon" to aid in scriptural interpretation and application. That process is helpful to the larger church when the choice of an organizing principle or of a "canon within the canon" is made clearly, on the basis of stated reasons, and when the conversation on the appropriate center for scriptural interpretation remains open.

A SECOND CLAIM

We have taken considerable space to evaluate the first claim of "canonical" interpreters of Scripture, the claim that the whole canon provides the context for scriptural interpretation in the church. We turn now to the second claim of such interpreters: Scripture *in its canonical form* provides the resource for faith and practice in the church.

In recent years considerable attention has been paid to tracing the prehistory of biblical texts. What history lies behind the scriptural traditions? What traditions were passed on by word of mouth within Israel or within the church? What were the earliest sources in which these traditions were written down? How were those sources combined, edited, and revised?

Canonical interpreters wish to suggest that these are valuable questions for reconstructing the prehistory of the biblical text, that they may provide helpful insights for the interpretation of the biblical text, but that it is the biblical text in its canonical (finished) form which is the resource for Christian reflection and action.

Among interpreters of Scripture we can find two different sorts of reasons for such claims. Some biblical scholars, like Brevard Childs, are especially concerned with the interpretation of Scripture for the church.

They insist that it is the church's Scripture, therefore, which ought to be interpreted. The church's canon includes the Gospel of Mark, but not an oral tradition of miracle stories, or a written passion narrative, or any other source which Mark might have used. The church's Scripture includes Exodus, but not its hypothetical sources, J, D, E, or P.

Other biblical interpreters have been impressed by "secular" literary critics who remind interpreters that it is exceedingly difficult to arrive with any certainty at an accurate description of the pre-history of any text. Further, say these literary critics, the purpose of interpretation is always to interpret the text at hand and not some reconstructed text of hypothetical pre-textual tradition.[36]

Similarly, Hans Frei suggests that in regard to the narrative portions of Scripture, historical-critical interpreters have made a fundamental mistake.[37] The significance of the narrative material in the Bible lies in the narratives themselves, and not in claims or hypotheses about the history which lies behind those narratives:

> By speaking of the narrative shape of these accounts, I suggest that what they are about and how they make sense are functions of the depiction or narrative rendering of the events constituting them—including their being rendered at least partially, by the device of chronological sequence.[38]
>
> But in effect, the realistic or history-like quality of biblical narratives, acknowledged by all, instead of being examined for the bearing it had in its own right on meaning and interpretation was immediately transposed into the quite different issue of whether or not the realistic narrative was historical.[39]

There is much that is persuasive in the arguments of such interpreters. It is Mark and not Ur-Mark or an oral tradition of conflict sayings or a reconstructed "life of Jesus" which the church recognizes as Scripture, and it is Mark which provides the lectionary texts for the church's lessons and sermons. It is Paul's letters and not the pre-Pauline hymns which are included in the church's liturgy.

Moreover, any reconstruction of hypothetical texts, sources, or traditions is, by definition, hypothetical. There is something comforting for the interpreter about being told that what he or she is asked to interpret is the text we have—not its reconstructed ancestor.

However, our discussion of the varieties of scriptural literature and the varieties of authority which such literature may claim cautions us against the assumption that there is only *one* appropriate locus for scriptural interpretation, the canonical form of the text.

For instance, our discussion of narrative in Chapter 3 suggests that within the canon itself distinctions are made between what we may call story and what we may call history. The reader or listener knows that there is a difference between the recounting of the incidents of Davidic kingship in the books of Samuel and the tale of Job in the Book of Job. The reader of the New Testament distinguishes between two different sorts of literary introduction:

a) "There was a man who had two sons, and the younger of them said to his father . . . " (Luke 15:11–12)

b) In the fifteenth year of the reign of Tiberius Caesar, Pontius Pilate being governor of Judea, and Herod being tetrarch of Galilee, and his brother Phillip tetrarch of the region of Ituraea . . . in the high-priesthood of Annas and Caiaphas, the word of God came to John the son of Zechariah in the wilderness . . . (Luke 3:1–2)

Both paragraphs introduce narratives, but the narratives are of different sorts. The first narrative says to the listener, "Now don't ask the name of the father and the two sons or where the family farm was. This is a story." The second narrative suggests to the listener, "That must have been around A.D. 29" and entices the listener to ask questions about historical setting. Obviously the difference between the two introductions is not that one introduces clear fiction and the other plain truth. It is rather more that the first introduction introduces a story which seems self-contained. The second introduction introduces a story which points behind itself and at least seems to make claims about history. Even in their canonical form, the two texts cannot be read in precisely the same way.

A similar question can be raised about the four canonical Gospels. Are they all the same type of literature? Is each best described as a realistic narrative, or are some of them closer to sermons, or legal collections, or to Hellenistic histories? Do the claims of any of the gospels about Jesus force us to look behind the Gospels at his history as far as we can know it?

The parables provide a further problem in narrative interpretation. What if a parable's context in the Gospel suggests more than one possible interpretation, and the interpretations are at least partly contradictory? (See for instance the endings of the parable of the Unjust Steward in Luke 16:1–13.) What if the interpretation of the parable provided by the canonical writer does not really fit the parable he relates? (See Mark 4:13–20 versus Mark 4:1–9.) Do these instances force the reader of the *canonical* material to raise the question of what lies behind the canonical form, what the parable looked like before Luke or Mark or the early church interpreted it?

Furthermore, Frei acknowledges that the narrative material comprises only part of the canon.[40] Do other kinds of literature force us to ask historical questions in ways that narrative material may not, force us behind the canonical forms? For example, do Paul's letters, with their strong note of polemic, force us to hypothetical reconstructions of the arguments in which he was engaged, even though our texts provide only *his* side of the argument? Or in dealing with legal or wisdom material, do we need to make some judgments about the social and historical circumstances out of which various prescriptions arose so that we can understand their possible application to our own perhaps very different social and historical circumstances?

All this leads us to suggest that at some points the canon itself encourages us to look behind the canon. All that we have said about the diversity of biblical literature would suggest that there is *no single way* to approach that literature which suffices in every instance. While the canonical form of the text obviously has a fundamentally important status in the church as the *starting* point for scriptural interpretation, preaching, and worship, that final canonical form sometimes points us to questions of what sources preceded the canonical text, and what history lies behind it.[41]

THE COMMUNITY AS THE CONTEXT FOR THE INTERPRETATION OF SCRIPTURE

Our emphasis on the importance of the canonical form of Scripture for the worship and preaching of the church leads us to make explicit what has been implicit in this chapter. Not only does the canon provide a fundamental resource for the church's faith and practice, the church provides the context in which the canon is interpreted. The Christian does not sit in splendid isolation reflecting on a scriptural text and seeking to apply it to his or her own life. Christians gather in communities where Scripture provides the basis for a sermon, a resource for study, a guide for action, and the basis of ongoing conversation.

Each form of Scripture we have discussed in the preceding chapters finds the fullest context for its interpretation within the community of faith. Scripture demonstrates its authority in diverse ways, to the individual believer and especially to the faithful Christian community.

In regard to those Scripture texts which deal most directly with the "words" of God, the church provides that context where the Word of God is still proclaimed, heard, and acknowledged. To be sure, the preacher's word is not that of the prophet or of the apostle. It is not a direct "thus says the Lord." The preacher's words rather interpret the words of the prophets and apostles, as well as the wisdom of the sages and the stories of the historians, for the lives of the community. But the preacher preaches and the people listen with the faith that God's word is still alive and active. The initial "Now hear this" can still be discerned speaking through Scripture. The Spirit who attested God's word to the prophets and apostles uses preachers and congregations and still summons people to assent, acceptance, and obedient faith.

Of course this discussion is meant to be suggestive rather than restrictive. Narrative and wisdom literature provide resources for the church's preaching as does the literature of proclamation. Parables, as well as proverbs, may provide clues for the church's ethical reflection.

The church is that community which retells and enacts the stories of God's deeds and of the deeds of faithful people. In sermon, song, drama, and especially in sacrament, the church re-enacts and appropriates the central moments of God's activity with humankind. From the simplest skit on a familiar parable to the liturgical richness of the Eucharist, the church not only retells the story, it relives the story. The church dares to claim Israel's history as the church's prehistory. The church dares to claim the apostles and disciples as the fathers and mothers of its faith, the forerunners of its own journey.

In its discussions and even in its board meetings, the church represents an arena where the wisdom of God is debated, discussed, received. As a people living in the world of hard facts and harder decisions, the church acknowledges the necessity for common sense—for practical sense, for shared sense. As a people of God, the church also acknowledges that such wisdom is part of the divine creation. Therefore the church appeals to common sense humbly and prayerfully, as a community.

Perhaps the church is preeminently the community of witness.[42] The church's central task is to bear witness to that mercy, love, hope, and judgment found in Jesus Christ. Our discussion of Scripture as witness suggests that the church, therefore, adds to the testimony of Scripture the testimony of its own experience. The church claims that its life sustains the claims of the Scripture which informs that life. The church trusts that as we declare the congruence between the claims of Scripture and the life we have found in Jesus Christ, others will be led to see that the light of God does shine in the face of this person. The church is that community where Christians witness to one another of Jesus Christ, thus sustaining one another in faith. The church is also that community which bears witness to the larger world. The church dares to say: Here is the mercy we have known. The Scripture we read, and the lives we live—in all their imperfection and through all their imperfection—bear witness to the mercy of God in Jesus Christ.

More than that, the church trusts Jesus Christ to bear witness to himself. Therefore the church speaks of him, knowing that faith comes only when he uses the church's witness to speak of himself.

Thus we end where we began. When God speaks to humankind it is *God* who speaks. No one can guarantee or limit the freedom and the power of God's speaking. The Bible cannot guarantee that speaking. The church cannot guarantee that speaking.

Yet the church acknowledges that God has spoken generation after generation through the words of the Bible. No analysis of the Bible's literature can predict with any certainty the times or the ways in which God will speak. Such analysis may, however, indicate that the Bible itself suggests that God speaks in many and diverse ways. Our study suggests that those who wait upon the Lord will do well to be aware of the varied ways in which God has addressed humankind through the Bible, and to listen eagerly for the varied ways in which God can use the Bible to address us still.

NOTES

1. Cf. David Dungan, "The New Testament Canon in Recent Study," *Int.* 29 (1975), 350, and Albert Sundberg, "The Making of the New Testament Canon," *The Interpreter's One-Volume Commentary on the Bible,* ed. Charles M. Laymon (Nashville: Abingdon Press, 1971), 1216–217.

2. Werner Georg Kümmel, *Introduction to the New Testament,* Eng. trans. Howard Clark Kee (Nashville: Abingdon Press, 1975), 505.

3. For a history of the New Testament canon, cf. Kümmel, *Introduction,* 475–510; Sundberg, *"New Testament Canon,"* 1216–24; and Hans von Campenhausen, *The Formation of the Christian Bible,* Eng. trans. John A. Baker (Philadelphia: Fortress Press; London: Adam and Charles Black, 1972).

4. Cf. von Campenhausen, *Formation,* 21.

5. For a parallel in the Gospel literature, cf. Mark 10:11–12.

6. Cf. von Campenhausen, *Formation,* 147–67.

7. Cf. Irenaeus, *Against Heresies,* III, xi, 8, in *The Ante-Nicene Fathers,* Vol. I, ed. A. Robertson and J. Donaldson (Grand Rapids: Wm. B. Eerdmans, 1956), 428, and von Campenhausen, *Formation,* 173.

8. Cf. von Campenhausen, *Formation,* 237.

9. I am not altogether persuaded by Sundberg's argument for a later date and Eastern location for the Muratorian Canon. See Albert Sundberg, "The Bible Canon and the Christian Doctrine of Justification," *Int.* 1975: 362–3. Even if Sundberg is right, however, my use of the Muratorian Canon is to illustrate the sorts of issues pertinent to Christian claims regarding authoritative scripture. The

date of the claims might be later, but the purport of the arguments remains the same.

10. Cf. The Muratorian Canon, 11. 5–9. on Luke and 11. 73–80. on Hermas, which was written too late to qualify for inclusion in the canonical list. (The Muratorian Canon can be found translated in Edgar Hennecke and Wilhelm Schneemelcher, *New Testament Apocrypha*, Eng. trans. R. McL. Wilson [Philadelphia: Westminster Press, 1963], I:42–45). Cf. also von Campenhausen, *Formation*, 254–59.

11. Cf. Muratorian Canon, 11. 45.

12. See Schubert Ogden's distinction between *de facto* and *de jure* authority in "Sources of Religious Authority in Liberal Protestantism," *JAAR* 44/3 (1976):405.

13. For an elaboration of this idea of canonicity, cf. Willi Marxsen, "Das Problem des neutestamentlichen Kanons aus der Sicht des Exegeten," in *Das Neue Testament als Kanon*, ed. Ernst Käsemann (Göttingen: Vandenhoeck and Ruprecht, 1970), 233–46. For its application to the Muratorian Canon (and the status of Hermas) see C. H. Dodd, *The Authority of the Bible* (New York: Harper & Row, Torchbooks, 1958), 3.

14. Cf. Brevard Childs on the canon of the Old Testament: "It is constitutive of Israel's history that the literature formed the identity of the religious community which in turn shaped the literature." See his *Introduction to the Old Testament as Scripture* (Philadelphia: Fortress Press, 1979), 41.

15. There are of course many places where the analogy breaks down. The Constitution is primarily a legal document. The canon includes legal material but much else as well. The Constitution is interpreted by lawyers in argument, while the canon is more often interpreted by preachers in sermons. (Though one should not underestimate the homiletical use of the Constitution, particularly in public school social studies classes.) The procedures for amending the Constitution are clearly stipulated in the Constitution itself; not so for the canon. The canon's authority is derived ultimately from the Word of God; the Constitution's authority is derived ultimately from the consent of the people.

16. Cf. Childs, *Introduction; Biblical Theology in Crisis* (Philadelphia: Westminster Press, 1970); and *The Book of Exodus*, OTL (Philadelphia: Westminster Press, 1974); James A. Sanders, *Torah and Canon* (Philadelphia: Fortress Press, 1972) and the various articles included in Ernst Käsemann, ed., *Das Neue Testament als Kanon* (Göttingen: Vandenhoeck and Ruprecht, 1970).

17. Cf. for example, Friedrich Mildenberger, "The Unity, Truth, and Validity of the Bible," *Int.* 29 (1975):29, 391–405. Hans Küng, "Der Frühkatholizismus im Neuen Testament als Kontroverstheologisches Problem," in *Das Neue Testament als Kanon*, ed. Käsemann, 175–204; Childs, *Exodus*, xvi; *Biblical Theology in Crisis*, 98–122.

18. See Gerhard von Rad, "Typological Interpretation of the Old Testament," in *Essays in Old Testament Hermeneutics*, ed. Claus Westermann, Eng. trans. James L. Mays (Atlanta: John Knox Press, 1979), 39.

19. For an overly simple but helpful summary of the problem, cf. Rudolph Bultmann, "Prophecy and Fulfillment," in *Essays in Old Testament Hermeneutics*, 50–75.

20. Cf. G. Ernest Wright and Reginald H. Fuller, *The Book of the Acts of God* (Garden City: Doubleday & Co., Anchor Books, 1960).

21. The last is what is called "typological" interpretation. Essays on these approaches are found in Claus Westermann, ed., *Essays in Old Testament Hermeneutics*, Eng. trans. James L. Mays (Atlanta: John Knox Press, 1979), and are questioned by James Barr in *Old and New in Interpretation* (New York: Harper & Row; London: SCM Press, 1966), 103–48. Cf. also Leonhard Goppelt, *Typos: The Typological Interpretation of the Old Testament in the New*, Eng. trans. Donald H. Madvig. (Grand Rapids: Wm. B. Eerdmans), 1982.

22. Childs undertakes such exegesis in his commentary on Exodus in *The Book of Exodus*, but he tends to restrict the discussion to New Testament texts which explicitly refer to the Exodus text under discussion. Other forms of interrelationship would also bear study.

23. Wright and Fuller, *The Book of the Acts of God*, xi.

24. See Walter Eichrodt, *Theology of the Old Testament*, OTL, Eng. trans. John Baker (Philadelphia: Westminster Press, 1967), 510–20.

25. See Samuel Terrien, *The Elusive Presence: Toward A New Biblical Theology*, RP (San Francisco: Harper & Row, 1978).

26. Martin Luther, "Preface to James and Jude," cited in B. A. Gerrish, "Biblical Authority and Reformation," *SJT* 10 (1957):343. See Martin Luther, *Works*, ed. Helmut T. Lehmann, vol. 35 ed. E. Theodore Bachmann, Eng. trans. Charles M. Jacobs (Philadelphia: Muhlenberg Press, 1960), 396.

27. Quoted by Ernst Käsemann, "Blind Alleys in the 'Jesus of History' Controversy," in *New Testament Questions of Today*, Eng. trans. W. J. Montague (Philadelphia: Fortress Press; London: SCM Press, 1969), 31. Cf. also the structure of Volume I of Jeremias's *New Testament Theology*. The volume is entitled "The Proclamation of Jesus," Eng. trans. John Bowden (New York: Charles Scribner's Sons; London: SCM Press, 1971). The task of this fundamental volume of the *Theology* is to reconstruct Jesus' history and teaching.

28. Käsemann, "Thoughts on the Present Controversy About Scriptural Interpretation," in *New Testament Questions*, 282.

29. Käsemann, "Thoughts on the Present Controversy," 277. Cf. also the remarks by Käsemann in *Das Neue Testament als Kanon*, 403–5.

30. Note how differently Jeremias and Käsemann can specify their understanding of what God has done in Christ.

31. Cf. Küng, "Der Frühkatholizmus" Küng, of course is really arguing against a canon within the canon and for the whole canon. Cf. my discussion.

32. Karl Barth, *Church Dogmatics*, I/2., Eng. trans. G. T. Thomson and Harold Knight (Edinburgh: T. & T. Clark, 1956), 599–600.

33. For a similar argument, cf. Kurt Aland, *The Problem of the New Testament Canon* (London: A. R. Mowbray and Co., 1962). We do not, however, conclude with Aland that we can or should undertake "the discovery of the correct principles of selection from the formal Canon and of its interpretation with the purpose of achieving a common, actual Canon and a common interpretation of its contents" (p. 31).

34. Cf. James B. Nelson, *Embodiment: An Approach to Sexuality and Christian Theology* (Minneapolis: Augsburg Publishing House, 1978), 181.

35. Nor is this exclusively a theoretical possibility. The late Edgar J. Goodspeed used to argue that Protestants should decide to include the Apocrypha as part of the Protestant canon.

36. Cf., for example, Roland M. Frye, "Literary Criticism and Gospel Criticism," *T Today* 36 (1979):207–19, and Frank Kermode, *The Genesis of Secrecy, On the Interpretation of Narrative* (Cambridge, Mass.: Harvard University Press, 1979), especially 138.

37. Hans Frei, *The Eclipse of Biblical Narrative: A Study in Eighteenth and Nineteenth Century Hermeneutics* (New Haven, Conn.: Yale University Press, 1974).

38. Frei, *Narrative*, 13.

39. Frei, *Narrative*, 16.

40. Frei, *Narrative*, 15.

41. The issue is further complicated by the fact that at some points Childs wants to distinguish between the canonical form and the final form of a text (cf. *Introduction*, 252, 498). Sanders relies in part on a reconstruction of another kind, the history of the self-understanding of Israel which led to the formation of the Canon (cf. *Torah and Canon*, xix–xx).

42. Karl Barth is eloquent in his portrayal of the church as a witnessing community. Cf., for example, *Church Dogmatics*, IV/3. Eng. trans. G. W. Bromiley (Edinburgh: T. & T. Clark, 1962), 843–53.

Index of Passages Cited

Index of Names

Abel, 71
Abraham, 7, 43, 59
Absalom, 43–44
Achtemeier, Paul, 3, 8
Adam, 43
Aland, Kurt, 153
Alexander, 54–55
Amaziah, 16, 18
Amos, 7, 16, 18, 21, 114
Auden, W. H., 66, 81
Augustine, 9, 80

Barr, James, 8–9, 11–12, 40, 153
Barth, Karl, 33, 40, 42, 49, 51, 80, 144, 153–54
Baruch, 20, 115, 127
Beardslee, William A., 111
Beker, J. Christiaan, 29, 42, 129
Betz, Hans Dieter, 111, 121, 129
Booth, Wayne, 34, 42
Briggs, C. A., 129
Bright, John, 25, 41, 116, 129
Brown, F., 129
Bultmann, Rudolf, 40, 49–51, 80, 152

Cain, 71
Calvin, John, 6, 9, 80, 145
Caulfield, Holden, 71–72
Childs, Brevard, 45, 79, 110, 136, 146, 152
Clements, R. E., 41
Coats, George W., 40, 110
Conzelmann, Hans, 79
Crossan, John Dominic, 80–81

Dahl, Nils, 51, 80
David, 7, 18, 43, 45–46, 48, 59, 61, 78
Dodd, C. H., 65, 80–81, 152
Driver, S., 129
Dungan, David, 151

Eichrodt, Walter, 140, 153
Elijah, 20
Eliot, T. S., 80
Elisha, 20
Eve, 43
Ezekiel, 13, 17, 20

Fowler, Robert M., 81
Frei, Hans, 48–51, 79–80, 147–48, 154
Friedrich, Gerhard, 42
Frye, Roland M., 154
Fuller, Reginald, 79, 140, 153
Funk, Robert, 120, 129

Gaius of Rome, 133
Gardner, Dame Helen, 7
Georgi, Dieter, 129
Gideon, 13
Good Samaritan, 72, 75–76, 80
Goodspeed, Edgar J., 154
Goppelt, Leonhard, 153
Grant, Jesse, 44
Grant, Ulysses S., 44–45, 47, 52–53, 79
Gray, Thomas, 110

Habel, Norman, 13–14, 40, 129
Hamlet, 2, 34, 66, 72–73
Hananiah, 24–26
Hennecke, Edgar, 152

159